HISTORY, LEGENDS & MYTHS

of

BEACON FALLS

MICHAEL A. KRENESKY

THE History PRESS

Published by The History Press
Charleston, SC
www.historypress.com

First published 2021

Manufactured in the United States

ISBN 9781467150613

Library of Congress Control Number: 2021943541

Notice: The information in this book is true and complete to the best of our knowledge. It is offered without guarantee on the part of the author or The History Press. The author and The History Press disclaim all liability in connection with the use of this book.

The history of Beacon Falls has long been a passion for my family, especially my parents, Michael and Beverly Krenesky.
They instilled in me that love for this community.

Their dedication toward keeping the history of Beacon Falls alive in the minds of all who would listen is the reason my father, the town's first official municipal historian, published a chronological history of Beacon Falls. It is why my mother, a former president of the Beacon Falls Historical Society, continually pushed for broader awareness of the historical society and its goal to collect and display the town's history, keeping it for future generations.

My wife, Joyce, and children have endured my rantings and ravings these many years as I searched for the details that are the history of Beacon Falls and finally became this book. To them, I have to say: thank you for listening and guiding me, as well as for leaving me locked in my porch office as I organized and finalized my thoughts.

And finally, there's the residents of Beacon Falls. Many say that Beacon Falls is a unique community that over the years has never lost its commitment to its neighbors. A local politician likened it to Brigadoon, something from the past that only surfaced every few years from the mist in the Naugatuck Valley.
We are all family.

To that end, I dedicate this brief history of Beacon Falls to all of you who are my family.

CONTENTS

PREFACE

As the town of Beacon Falls celebrated its 150th anniversary of incorporation on June 30, 2021, I compiled several short facts and stories associated with the town's history. Much of this history predates the incorporation, but nevertheless, it is the flavor and color that laid the foundation for the town to build and grow as it has.

I hope that this small work will enlighten you on the history of Beacon Falls and that it will not only answer some of your questions about the town but also open you to more questions and begin your own historical journey.

The town of Beacon Falls, Connecticut, which was incorporated on June 30, 1871, celebrated its sesquicentennial anniversary on June 30, 2021. After 150 years of change and progress, it remains one of the smallest towns in the state and is the fifth youngest behind West Haven (1921), Ansonia (1889), Thomaston (1875) and Newington (July 1871).

As Beacon Falls begins its 150th year, the town's origins are information that the curious want to understand. Many have read about Beacon Falls being incorporated through taking land from the towns of Bethany (incorporated 1832), Naugatuck (1844), Oxford (1798) and Seymour (1850), but few have the deeper knowledge of our earliest beginnings. It is not my intent to go into the full history that is the Naugatuck Valley and the larger picture that is the state of Connecticut, but rather to establish a foundation that might inspire the reader to do this research themselves.

In addition, as I might reference some Native American history, which admittedly is not in my limited area of expertise, I ask for the latitude to do so while acknowledging that it may need further fact checking.

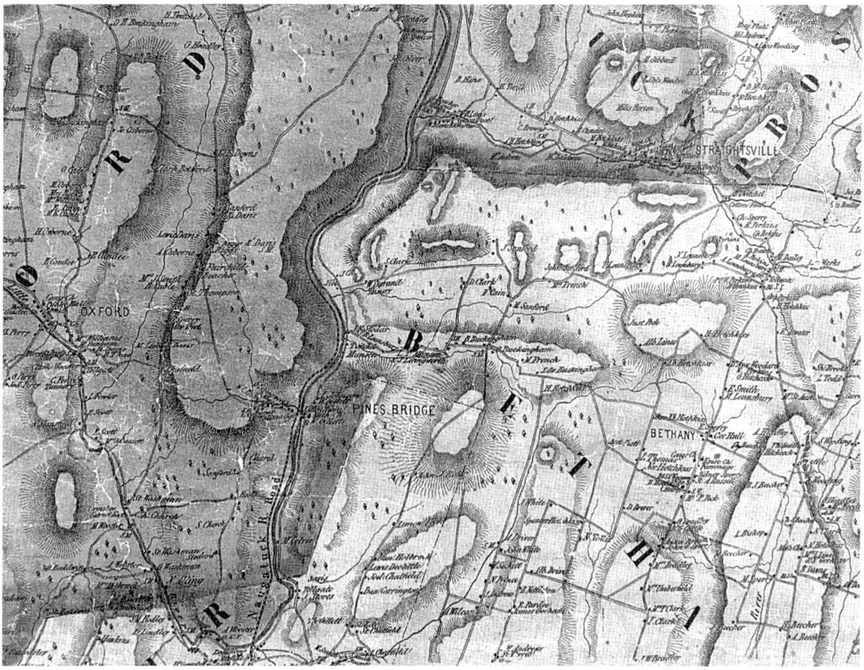

1852 *Map of Bethany*, the area that would become Beacon Falls in 1871. *Courtesy of the Beacon Falls Historical Society.*

This history will only reference tribes from Western Connecticut and the Naugatuck Valley.

Compiled in the following pages are the research and published works from several sources. Where I can best identify an author, I have done so. By pulling this information into a single place, I hope that the reader will also acknowledge that our history is more complicated than perhaps originally understood, and by publishing it here again, I hope to pay homage to where we have come from, as this is the basis to understanding where we may need go to in the future.

The stories I have included are all related to Beacon Falls history. While much of it occurred before the town's incorporation in 1871, it is all part of where and how the town of Beacon Falls was born.

Opposite: View of the "hill" section, Highland Avenue, Maple Avenue, Division Street and Top Notch Field. *Courtesy of the Beacon Falls Historical Society.*

ORIGIN OF THE COLONY OF CONNECTICUT

The story of Beacon Falls has to begin somewhere, and that place is the Massachusetts Bay Colony in March 1630. As more people came from England, they began to explore the area we now call Boston. Several settlements were established at Dorchester and Watertown. Circa 1635, a group of these settlers petitioned to expand out into the wilderness west of the colony, and once this was granted, they relocated to the Connecticut River

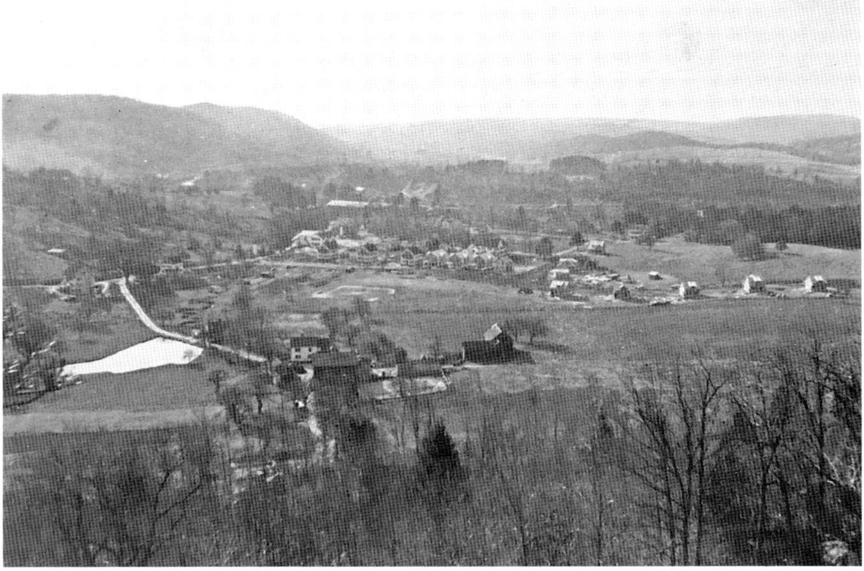

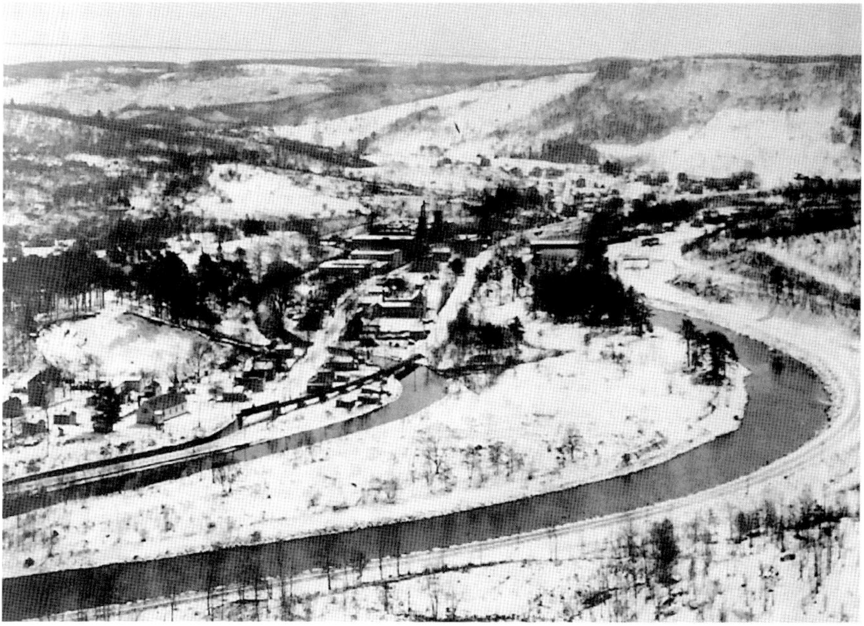

Beacon Falls, 1931. *Courtesy of the Beacon Falls Historical Society.*

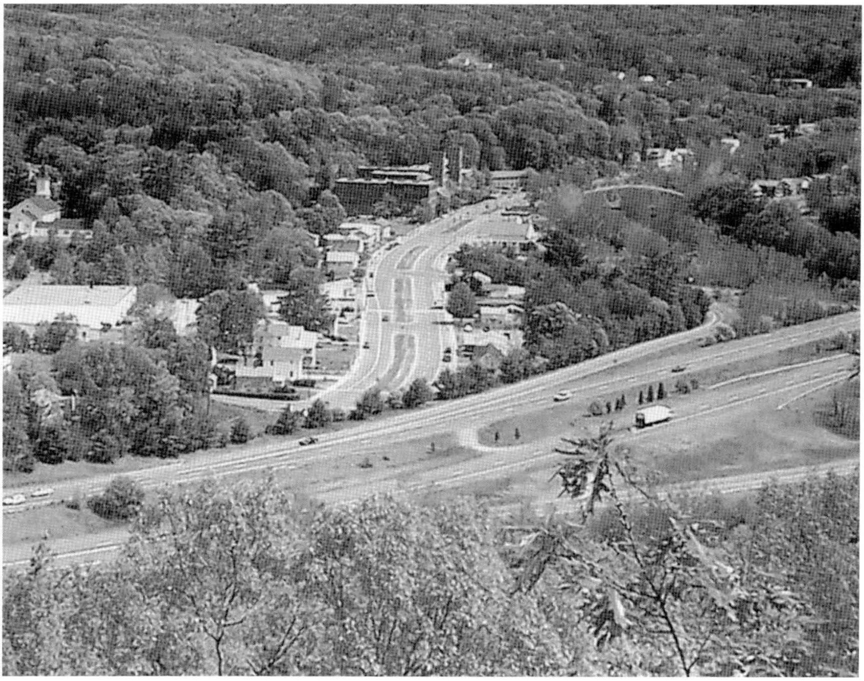

Beacon Falls, 1988. *Courtesy of the Beacon Falls Historical Society.*

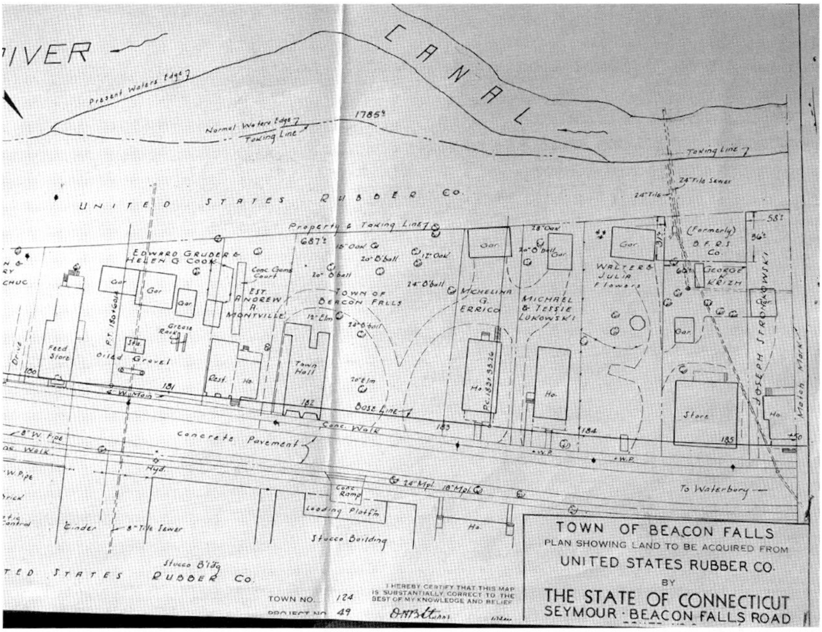

Plan of Upper North Main Street, circa 1940. *Courtesy of the Town of Beacon Falls, Public Records.*

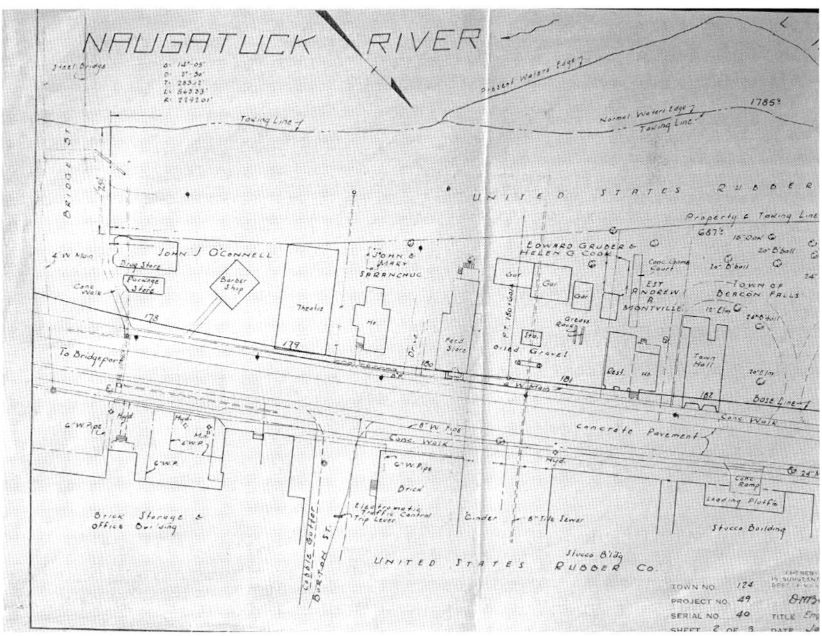

Plan of Lower North Main Street, circa 1940. *Courtesy of the Town of Beacon Falls, Public Records.*

and established the first towns that would become Hartford, Wethersfield and Windsor. Others would come, and the exploration of Connecticut took them to the southern coastline.

Where does Beacon Falls fall into the early history of Connecticut? It begins with the settlement of the New Haven Colony around 1638 and the expansion into the lands immediately to the west of that colony.

The following chronological timeline of the settlement of Connecticut, specifically the towns that make up the Naugatuck Valley, led to the incorporation of Beacon Falls in 1871. The lands just south of what is now considered to be the Lower Naugatuck Valley began with the settlement of the town of Stratford in 1639.

1620–1630	Massachusetts Bay Colony
1634	Hartford Area (Windsor, Wethersfield, Hartford) from the Massachusetts Bay Colony
1638	New Haven
1639	Stratford
1639	Milford
1651	Derby
1674	Waterbury
1787	Southbury
1798	Oxford from Derby and Southbury (Oxford Parish, 1741)
1832	Bethany from Woodbridge, which itself was incorporated in 1784 from Milford (Bethany Parish, 1762)
1844	Naugatuck from Bethany, Oxford, and Waterbury
1850	Seymour from Derby
1871	Beacon Falls from Bethany, Oxford, Naugatuck, Seymour

NATIVE AMERICAN HISTORY

WESTERN CONNECTICUT

The Native American tribes that lived and hunted Western Connecticut were many, and any attempt on my part to accurately list them will be lacking, so I am going to refer to two sources from prominent authors and historians of the time, Samuel Orcutt (1824–1893) and John William De Forest (1826–1906). The books referenced are De Forest's *History of the Indians of Connecticut from the Earliest Known Period to 1850* (1851) and Orcutt's *Indians of the Housatonic and Naugatuck Valleys* (1882).

Orcutt lists in some detail the names of tribes and, more specifically, the huge number of land sales that transpired between these tribes and the early settlers. Note that landownership was a new concept to Native Americans. Yes, they held "territory," but the reality was that there was no firm border as we know them today between Native American tribal lands. There are several stories that form the basis of several myths. They touch on the issue of slavery—for some, this history may be difficult to acknowledge, but there is no hiding from it, only learning from it.

De Forest's five-hundred-page volume on Connecticut's Native American history is noted as one of the most comprehensive on this topic. It is a go-to reference for someone researching Connecticut Native American history. It covers manners and customs and goes into detail on the chronological history that is Connecticut's Native American heritage.

There is also the topic of slavery in Connecticut. The story of the enslaved Native American man Toby (properly spelled "Tobe") is an important piece of Beacon Falls history. The town dedicated an area,

Toby's Pond, to him in 2009. To understand the relevance of this story to our history, consider these comments found in Bernard Steiner's 1893 work, *History of Slavery in Connecticut*:

> *In Connecticut, as in many other States, the first slaves were not of African race, but were aborigines, taken in battle and sold as slaves, in the same manner as the Anglo-Saxon forefathers of the early settlers had sold the captives of their spear, over a millennium before. After the fierce and bloody Pequod War, the colonists found on their hands a number of captive Indians, whose disposition formed a pressing question. It did not take long to decide it. To the shame of the conquerors, "Ye prisoners were divided, some to those of the River* [Connecticut] *and the rest to us" of Massachusetts.*

The formal abolition of slavery in Connecticut did not happen until 1848. During the years from 1640 to 1848—most specifically up to 1774, when the "Non-Importation Act" was adopted—opinions on slavery gradually changed. Between 1774 and 1830, the abolitionist movement gained a foothold—the extinction of slavery in Connecticut was ensured. The passage of the Fifteenth Amendment to the U.S. Constitution brought slavery in the state to a close at last.

The Story of Dinah

The following topic may lead to another discourse, but it is a part of our history. At first, you may not understand why it is even referenced here in a history of Beacon Falls, but the people mentioned in the story lived in and were the early settlers for the area that became Beacon Falls.

The early history of Connecticut is sometimes not what we all want to acknowledge, but it is fact. The expansion into Connecticut brought with it several encounters with its Native American inhabitants, and the resulting outcomes were war and slavery.

Samuel Orcutt covered this difficult issue in his book. The sale of land was a hard concept for Native Americans to grasp, and they may have thought that the land, once given, would revert back to them at some point. Early settlers, once they had the land, began to take more as many more settlers came to North America. This led to war, as well as the enslavement and selling of Native Americans.

In Orcutt's book, he referenced a deed dated June 8, 1722, in Stratford, Connecticut, wherein a Joseph Gorham, for the price of "sixty-pound money," sold to Colonel Ebenezer Johnson of Derby one Indian girl named Dinah, twenty-six years old. Ebenezer Johnson was the first settler in what is called Pinesbridge (spelled "Pines Bridge" in early documents) and the Nyumph section, which was the portion of Bethany that became Beacon Falls in 1871.

Six years later, in November 1728, after Johnson died, his estate was disposed of by his wife, Hannah Johnson, with a portion given to their son Timothy Johnson, and this included Dinah: "[G]ive, grant, and confirm unto my beloved son, Timothy Johnson, him, his heirs and assigns forever; that is to say, one Indian woman Dinah, and also a feather bed."

Orcutt went on to add his own admonition of slavery: "At no time in the history of American Slavery has the recognition of human beings as chattel been more complete than it is in this old document, in which 'the Indian woman Dinah' and 'the feather bed' are classified together in so unceremonious a way."

The story of Dinah is further relevant due to another account of Colonel Ebenezer Johnson's earlier interactions with the business of slavery: the story of Tobe (or "Toby," as the name was anglicized in today's language).

The Story of Toby (Tobe)

Thirty-seven years before the story of Dinah's enslavement, in 1676, Colonel Ebenezer Johnson took Toby as his slave. The story is told that Johnson was serving in the militia and was sent to the New London area during the King Philip's War. The day following a skirmish, Colonel Johnson was walking the battlefield when a young Indian boy ran up to him, fell at his feet and grabbed ahold of the colonel's leg. Johnson decided to keep the boy and took him as his slave. This was how Toby ended up in Beacon Falls. The story goes on that after twelve years, Johnson freed Toby in 1688. In a note in his own hand dated October 6, 1713, Johnson wrote a letter certifying that Toby was freed years before. It is unclear why this certification was needed, but it has been suggested that Toby was being challenged over the ownership of land he purchased. Orcutt commented in his book: "If the town recognized the land deeds from the Indians to the town as valid and good, why would it not also be true of the land deed to Toby?" Land records in Derby title the land as "Toby Indian's purchase" or "Toby's Land."

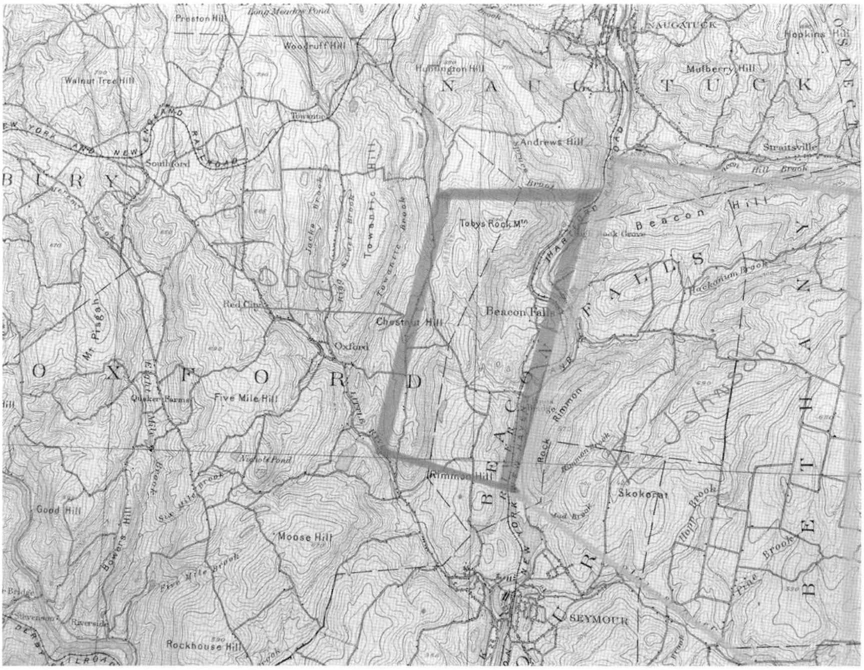

Map showing both Tobe's and Ebenezer Johnson's properties, parts of which would become Beacon Falls. *Courtesy of the Beacon Falls Historical Society.*

As recognition of the 125th anniversary of the town in 1996, a proclamation was created. In this document, Ebenezer Johnson's original land deed is cited as the land area from which parts would become Beacon Falls. To expand on this, on the image of the 1893 map here, the approximate locations of both Johnson's land (which became part of Bethany) and Toby's parcel (which became part of Oxford) are marked. The primary site of the town of Beacon Falls would be created from these two plots.

Upon Toby's death, Ebenezer Johnson's son Timothy Johnson was the main beneficiary and was willed the land from Rimmon Hill to High Rock. As mentioned, this area would ultimately be incorporated as the eastern boundary of Oxford when it was annexed from the town of Derby in 1798. It should be noted that at incorporation, Derby's northern border was at Beacon Hill Brook, which was at the time the southern boundary of Waterbury.

Toby purchased this area of land from the "Naugatuck Indians" in 1693. As described by Samuel Orcutt and highlighted in the attached map, the land spanned the area from Chestnut Tree Hill and Lopus Rocks to the

Naugatuck River to Beacon Hill Brook, west to the Little River and south to the Rimmon Hill and Rimmon Hill Rock, as well as the upper Rimmon Hill and the area known as Lopus Plain. Today, High Rock State Park in the Naugatuck State Forest is still known as Toby's Rock. Toby paid ten pounds and a barrel of cider for this property. Toby is the first person to own this land by deed.

Orcutt identified the Ebenezer Johnson parcel as located "in a place called Nayumps, bounded northerly by with Beacon Hill River, easterly with Milford, westerly by the Naugatuck River, south with Lebanon River."

The writings from Ebenezer Johnson suggest that Toby was a Mohegan. Other accounts, specifically the deed for the land purchase from the Naugatuck Indians by Toby, name him a Narragansett.

THE HISTORY OF THE MILL COMPLEX

EARLY 1800s TO 1935

The Mill Complex has always been perceived to be the "center" of Beacon Falls. Before 1850, John Coe owned a tannery that was located along the brook that runs today along the back of the property. In October 1937, George E. Bronson, a self-described historian, documented in a brief history of the Bronson Company that Coe turned over his business to his sons, John and Julius. Around 1850–51, the American Hard Rubber Company purchased the property, with the Coe Tannery moving farther south on Main Street to Lebanon Brook (known today as Hockanum Brook), which is the location of the old Bronson Company factory. The tannery produced leather products such as belts and laces until circa 1876, when it shut down.

The American Hard Rubber Company, which made products out of vulcanized rubber and was associated with Charles Goodyear, who lived in Naugatuck, remained on the site until 1853, when it was moved to College Point, Long Island. The company was owned by Conrad Poppenhusen, who became well known within the rubber industry. The Novelty Rubber Company was established in 1853, and it also moved its manufacturing out of Beacon Falls to New Jersey in 1855.

Replacing the Novelty Rubber Company in 1953, the Beacon Dam Company was established at the mill site. It operated in Beacon Falls until 1859, when Poppenhusen bought the company and moved it to College Point in 1861.

In researching the Beacon Dam Company, James E. Haas in his book, *Conrad Poppenhusen: Life of a German American Industrial Pioneer*, stated that the American Hard Rubber Company was originally named the Beacon Dam

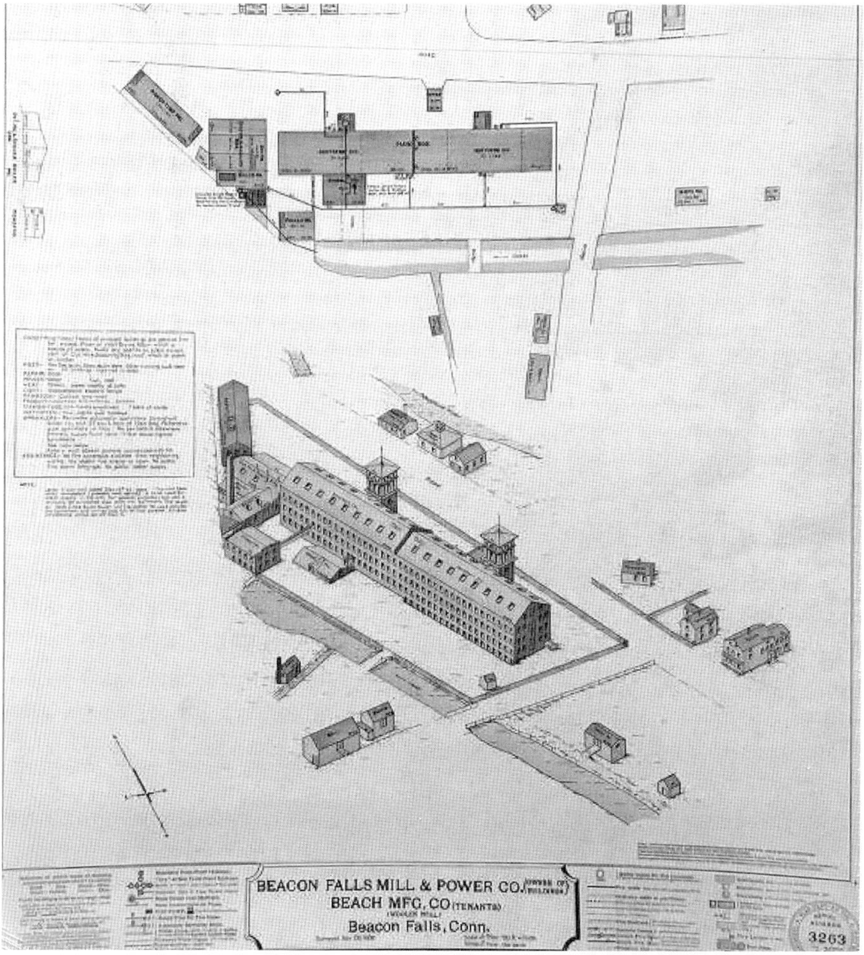

Illustration of Beacon Falls Mill & Power Company. *Courtesy of the Connecticut Historical Society.*

Company; due to a suit contested in the New York Supreme Court, the factory in Beacon Falls was renamed the American Hard Rubber Company. As noted, Conrad Poppenhusen purchased the American Hard Rubber Company and finalized its move to College Point, Long Island.

In 1863, the Home Woolen Company established itself at the mill. Much of the early building expansion was driven by the Home Woolen Company, and in 1867, a second building was erected. These buildings are where the two towers are located. When the Home Woolen Company moved operations out of Beacon Falls, Standard Woolen Company took root. The woolen business was changing rapidly during these years, and the Standard Woolen

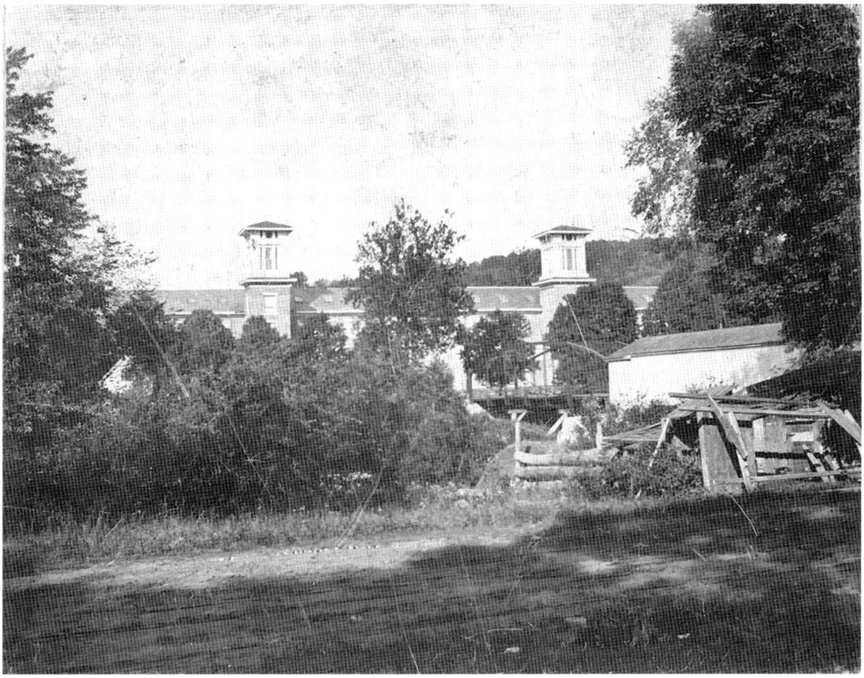

Beacon Falls Mill & Power Company. Postcard circa 1860s. *Author's collection.*

Company eventually closed. The Mill Complex is registered in the National Register of Historic Places as the site of the Home Woolen Company.

The buildings remained empty for several years until the Beacon Mill & Power Company purchased the structures. Beacon Mill & Power owned the buildings until 1898, when the Beacon Falls Rubber Shoe Company was established by George Lewis and his son, Tracy S. Lewis. The Lewis family had deep roots in Naugatuck and many of the businesses there, as did the Whittemore family.

A *Naugatuck Daily News* article dated August 23, 1898, noted that Harris Whittemore of Naugatuck purchased the mill property and may have been an investor, perhaps as a silent partner, in the ownership of the Beacon Falls Rubber Shoe Company. The article notes that Harris Whittemore purchased the deed of the Mill Complex for a price less than the $100,000 asking price. Whittemore refused to disclose what would be manufactured at the mill. There is also no reference to Harris Whittemore in any of the known histories of the Beacon Falls Rubber Shoe Company.

NAUGATUCK RAILROAD'S HIGH ROCK GROVE PICNIC GROUNDS

High Rock Grove was the most prominent attraction and feature of the lower Naugatuck Valley for more than two decades. Read here the history of the "Grove" as described by the owners of the area, the Naugatuck Railroad. This history is taken from a booklet produced by the Naugatuck Railroad/High Rock Grove marketing group. This booklet was a compilation of several sources, including the works of Samuel Orcutt and William De Forest.

With the completion of the Naugatuck Railroad in the year 1849, it made the valley accessible and brought notice to the public, both outside and within Connecticut, of one the most picturesque valleys in all New England. It was the Naugatuck River, which is one of the largest tributaries of the Housatonic River, that was instrumental in making the Naugatuck Valley thrive with manufacturing of textiles, rubber, brass and copper factories.

The Naugatuck River is roughly forty miles of twisting stretches and fantastic vistas. As noted by the railroad, one sees

> *rounded hills covered with woods, bluffs crowned with handsome residences, lofty crags built of primitive granite, verdurous meadows and busy manufacturing villages, as the visitor is borne northward and southward upon the winding track of the Naugatuck Railroad.*

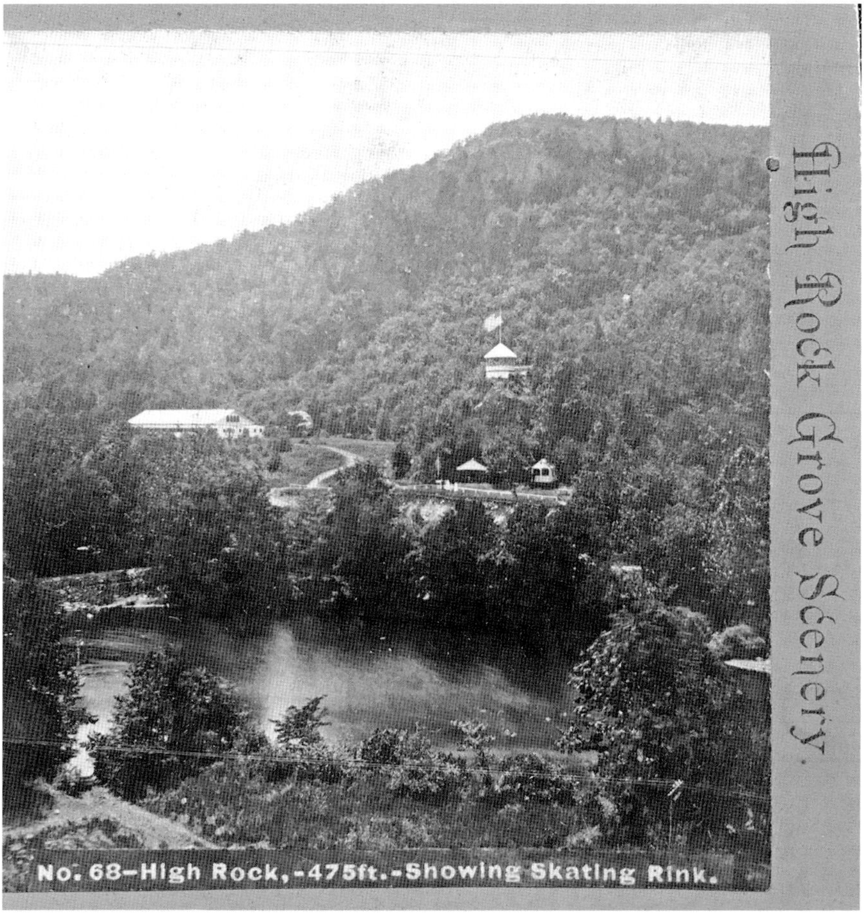

Above: Photo of High Rock Grove, circa 1910. *Author's collection.*

Opposite, top: Naugatuck Railroad's High Rock Grove marketing booklet. *Author's collection.*

Opposite, bottom: Photo of "Spruce Brook," which flowed from the top of High Rock, 1880. *Author's collection.*

There are many points of interest in the upper and lower divisions of the Valley...but of this whole romantic region the most impressive section is that which lies between the villages of Naugatuck and Seymour, or, more precisely, between the mouth of Beacon Hill Brook, which was mentioned earlier as the southernmost boundary of Waterbury, and the village of Beacon Falls.

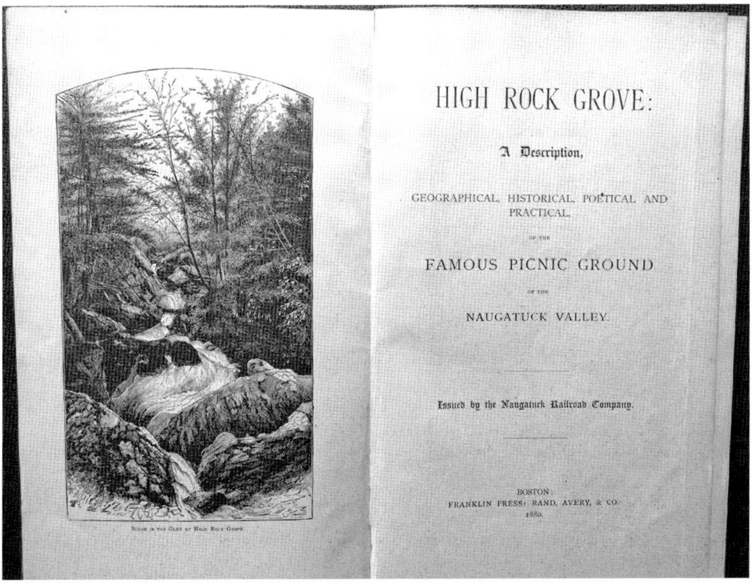

Scene in the Glen at High Rock Grove.

HIGH ROCK GROVE:

A Description,

GEOGRAPHICAL, HISTORICAL, POETICAL AND PRACTICAL,

OF THE

FAMOUS PICNIC GROUND

OF THE

NAUGATUCK VALLEY.

Issued by the Naugatuck Railroad Company.

BOSTON:
FRANKLIN PRESS: RAND, AVERY, & CO.
1880.

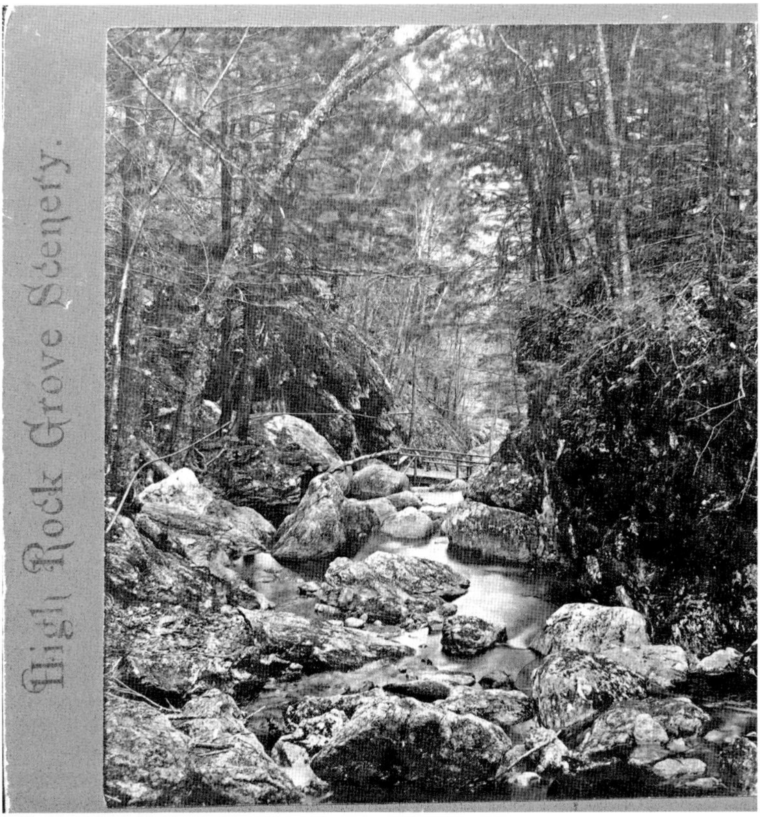

> *In the heart of the rugged area just mentioned on the West side of the Naugatuck River, is a narrow-wooded ravine through which plunges a mountain stream called Sherman's Brook. North and South of the brook, extends a range of hills, or rather, a lofty and precipitous ledge of rocks crowding the river on the North, but sweeping away from the river to the South. This area is named "High Rock," and the open space, "High Rock Glen." Below this space is a level strip of land that was once covered with a thick grove of trees, which at this writing is called "High Rock Grove."*
>
> *The Glen lies a mile North of Beacon Falls Village and approximately fifteen miles from New Haven and Bridgeport. With the craggy hills on both sides of the river, the reflection off the river is a picture that a true artist might take unmeasured delight. Facing the Glen, one must notice the high cliffs that frame the Glen. To the left is the aforementioned "Toby's Rock," and to the right, "Squaw Rock."*

This text appears to have been written by someone working for the Naugatuck Railroad. At this point, it appears that the Naugatuck Grove write-up take some passages directly from Samuel Orcutt's book. This goes on for several pages within the railroad's booklet. Included are the stories of Colonel Ebenezer Johnson, Toby and the related land purchases of both, referenced earlier herein.

High Rock Grove was a favorite retreat for many in Connecticut and neighboring states. It was not lost on its visitors that the Naugatuck Railroad was both an entrepreneur and nature conservationist. At a time when towns were expanding and destroying the forestland around them, High Rock Grove was a haven for those seeking the solitude of nature but also wishing for other entertainment options. Comments attributed to those who had visited the Grove describe this appreciation that the railroad understood the binding between people and nature. One visitor wrote in 1878:

> *Most places of this character are improved until they are quite spoiled—until nature is lost sight of in art that does not adorn; but with singular good taste the managers of High Rock Grove have preserved as nearly as possible all the natural beauties of the place.*

Other comments included, "It is as fresh as a new Eden.…The Naugatuck Railroad Company have done the public a beautiful service in buying up this heart of the Switzerland of Connecticut."

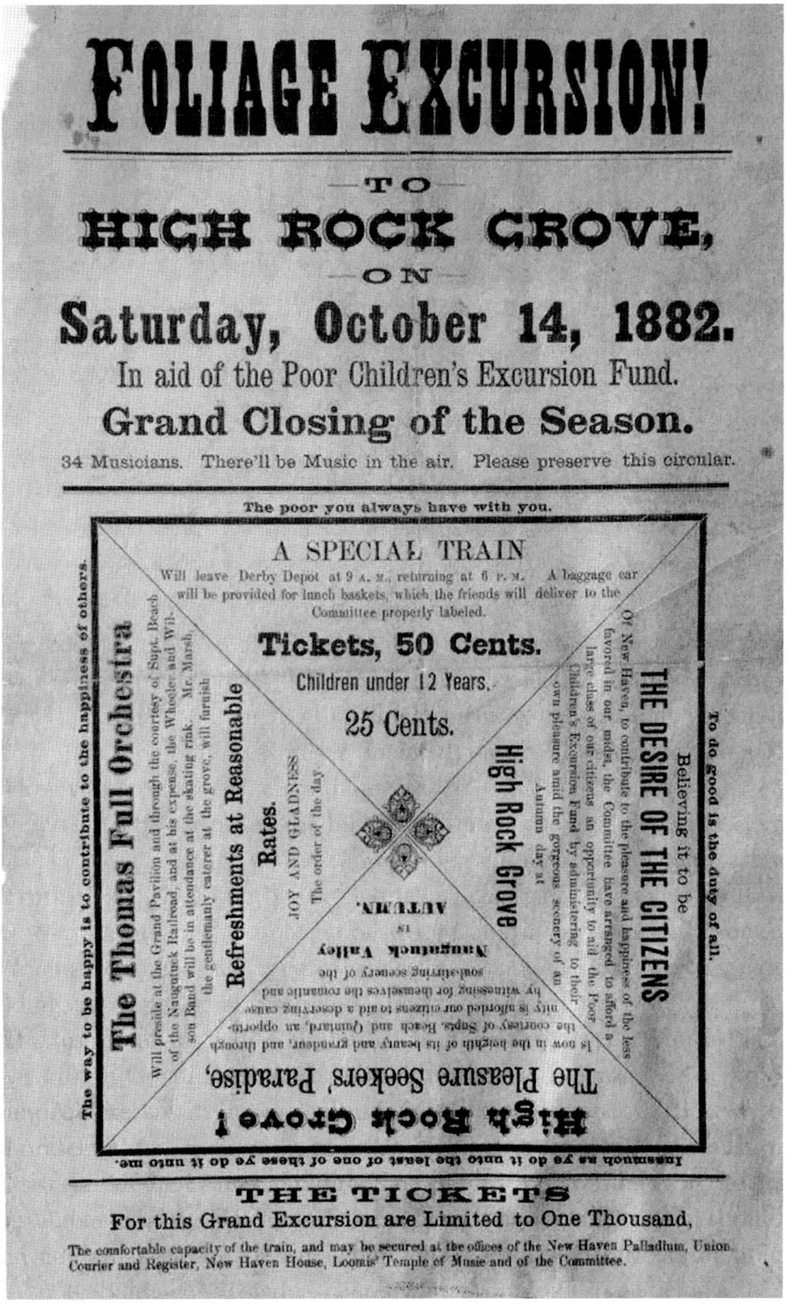

Advertisement for High Rock Grove train excursion, 1882. *Courtesy of the Connecticut Historical Society.*

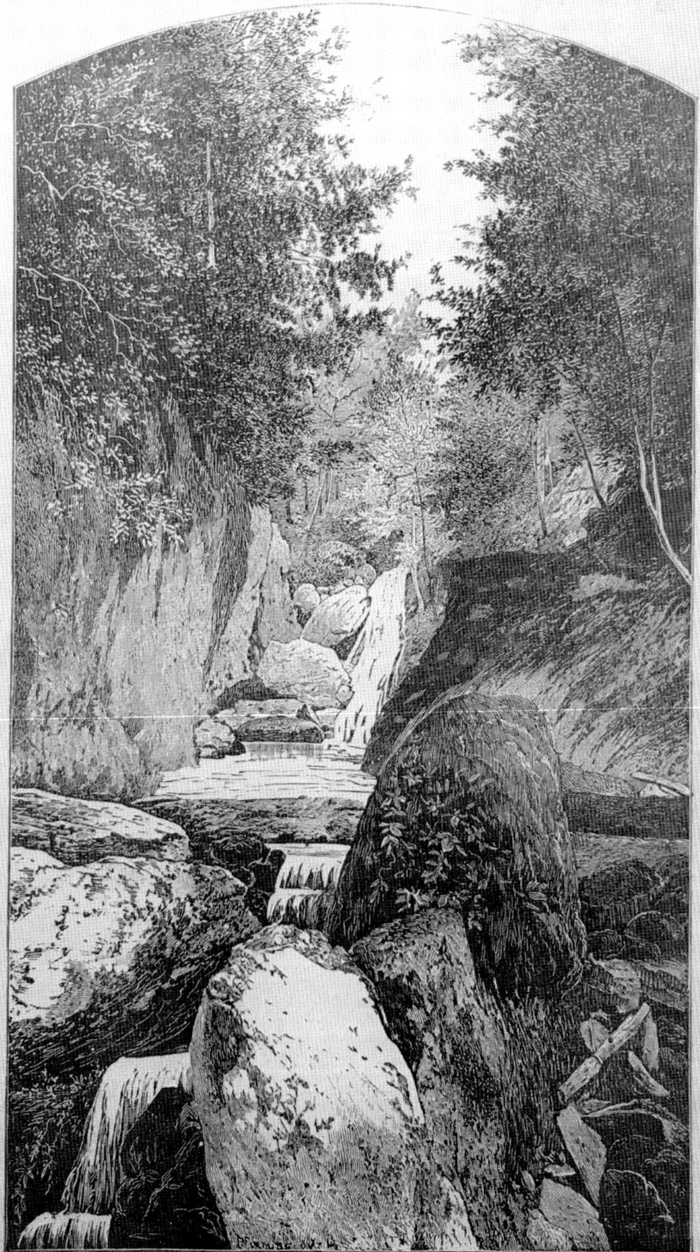

Scene in the Gorge at High Rock Grove on Naugatuck Railroad.

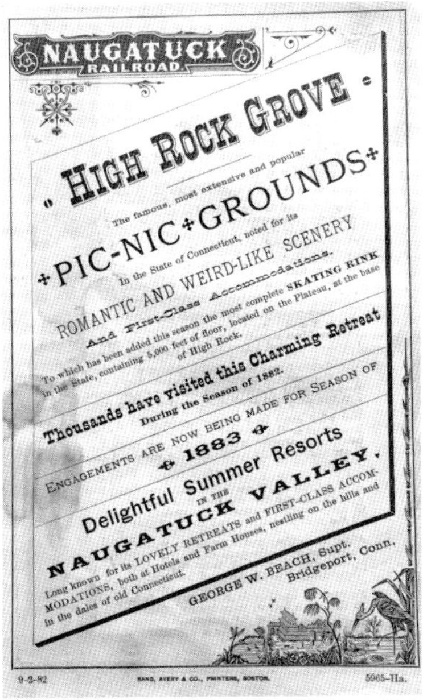

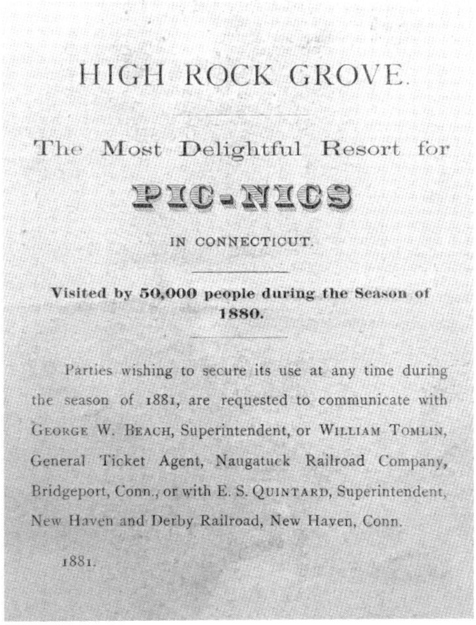

HIGH ROCK GROVE.

The Most Delightful Resort for

PIC-NICS

IN CONNECTICUT.

Visited by 50,000 people during the Season of 1880.

Parties wishing to secure its use at any time during the season of 1881, are requested to communicate with George W. Beach, Superintendent, or William Tomlin, General Ticket Agent, Naugatuck Railroad Company, Bridgeport, Conn., or with E. S. Quintard, Superintendent, New Haven and Derby Railroad, New Haven, Conn.

1881.

Opposite: Advertisement booklet for High Rock Grove, 1883. *Author's collection.*

Above, left: Advertisement postcard by the Naugatuck Railroad for High Rock Grove, photo circa 1881. *Author's collection.*

Above, right: Reverse of advertisement postcard. *Author's collection.*

Another noted:

> *High Rock Grove was opened ca. 1880 and closed around 1900. During its approximately 20 years of operation, it entertained nearly ten thousand people every summer. It was open seven-days a week with weekends being its busiest days. Besides its call to nature, at its peak, there was a 6,500 sq foot skating rink, it had a restaurant that served meals to those that did not bring a picnic lunch. The dam in the river, which was the headwater for the canal that brought water to the Mills to run the waterwheel that created both steam and eventually electric power, held back enough water for canoes and rowboats to be used on the river.*

The Grove closed as a resort shortly after the New Haven Railroad, also called the "Consolidated," purchased the Naugatuck Railroad. The Consolidated apparently was not interested in running a "park," although it was noted that people's attitudes and interests were changing at the turn of the century; as trolley lines were extended to other parts of the state, people had more destinations and attractions to capture their time.

In 1905, a fire destroyed the skating rink. Oddly, the Consolidated Railroad rebuilt the rink only to remove it five years later when the railroad tracks were relocated closer to the river.

In 1910, a forest fire razed the original caretaker's house and a barn built on the property, which was used as a farm for a short period of time.

In an article published on December 2, 1962, in the "Weekly Section" of the *Sunday Waterbury Republican* and written by Joseph Stephens, he closed his article as follows: "Passage of the years and the dearth of written information about the most extensive and popular pic-nic grounds in the State of Connecticut has taken the memory of High Rock Grove a long way along the road to its inevitable destination—oblivion."

In 1971, a bill was introduced and approved to rename the area after State Representative Clara O'Shea (D) of Beacon Falls. O'Shea was a conservationist years ahead of her time, working to save open space like High Rock Grove for future generations. Signage was created and posted, but time has also taken this away.

The former Grove area and its hiking trails are now known only as the Naugatuck State Forest, with no reference to High Rock Grove or to State Representative O'Shea.

EDUCATION IN BEACON FALLS

RIMMON SCHOOLHOUSE

The Rimmon one-room schoolhouse, which today sits near the corner of RT 42 (Pinesbridge Road) and Rimmon Hill Road, was established circa 1779 or 1830. The actual date of this specific building is the question.

The town of Derby created a school in the northern part of its then boundary circa 1779. References to the "Rimmon District" and the schoolhouse are not totally clear, and it is possible that the original building may have been in a different location. Oxford built or refurbished six schoolhouses circa 1830. Our schoolhouse resides in District No. 6 of the Oxford school system, and therefore, the Rimmon Schoolhouse may be one of those six schools.

For a number of years, there have been discussions to save the Rimmon Schoolhouse, as it is currently in disrepair, and the current owner has plans for the property. Over time, several efforts were started to relocate the schoolhouse. Currently, as of this writing, there is another effort regarding moving and renovating the current building on a site on North Main Street. The condition of the building is a concern; therefore, it may be more appropriate to build a replica integrating original parts of the building that can possibly be saved. Fundraising efforts by the Beacon Falls Historical Society through a "Buy a Brick" program is ongoing. The overall cost to relocate the building, including site preparation and construction, notwithstanding any volunteer labor and donations, is estimated to be well

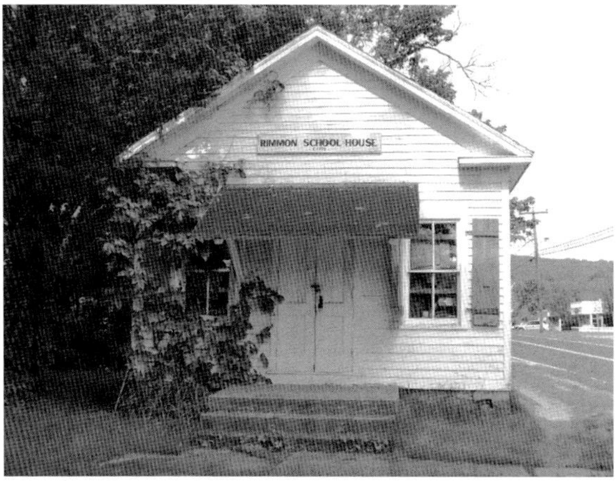

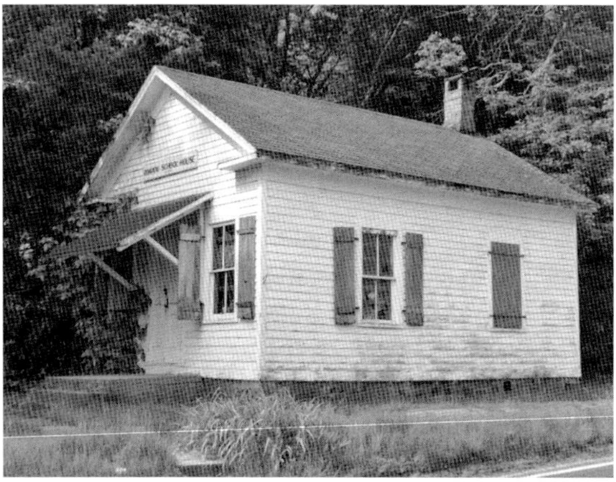

Top: Front view of the one-room Rimmon Schoolhouse. *Photo by author.*

Bottom: Side view of the Rimmon Schoolhouse. *Photo by author.*

over $50,000. It is not known if this cost will be so unaffordable that funding will not be forthcoming to save the building.

The Rimmon one-room schoolhouse is listed in the State Register of Historic Places.

Nyumph Schoolhouse

The Nyumph one-room schoolhouse was the second of three school buildings that serviced the children of Beacon Falls prior to 1955. Where the Rimmon Schoolhouse was located in Oxford, this school building was located in Bethany on the corner of Bethany Road and what is today Buckingham Drive. The school was very small, and when the school population outgrew the building, it was abandoned; a new one-room Nyumph school was built

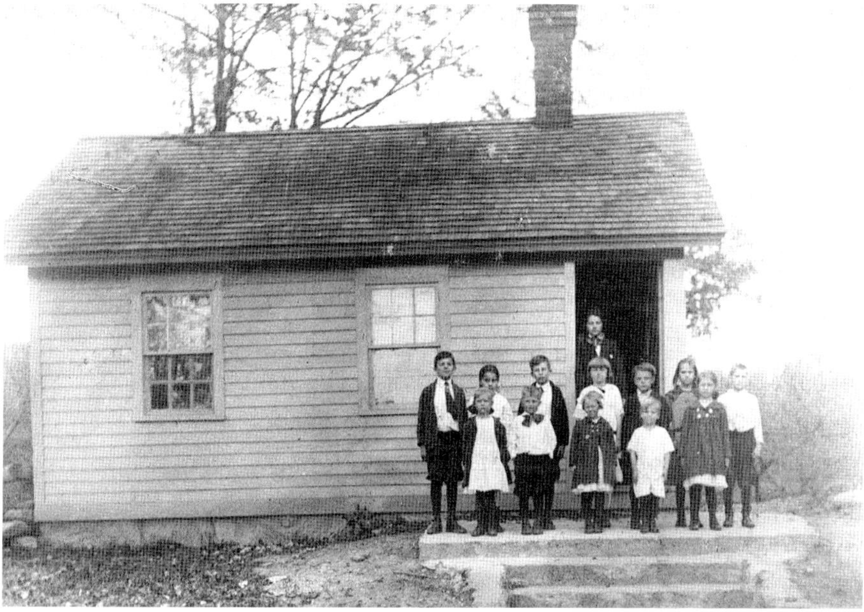

Photo of the one-room Nyumph schoolhouse that was on Burton Road. *Author's collection.*

on what today is Feldspar Avenue. The historical society does not have any photos of the Feldspar School, but it was renovated into a house that is located at 159 Feldspar Avenue. The original Nyumph Schoolhouse was also renovated into a single-family home.

Center School

Center School was the largest of the three schoolhouses in Beacon Falls and was located on College Avenue between Highland and Maple Avenues. At some point, College Avenue was renamed Burton Road—that date has not been verified. Different than the one-room schoolhouses, this building was a two-story wooden structure.

As the school population grew, the original wooden structure was expanded with a brick addition (circa 1922). In addition, Center School eventually housed the first Beacon Falls Public Library. The original wooden structure was torn down after the opening of Laurel Ledge Elementary School in 1954. The brick portion of the building saw new life, as it was renovated and today is the town hall.

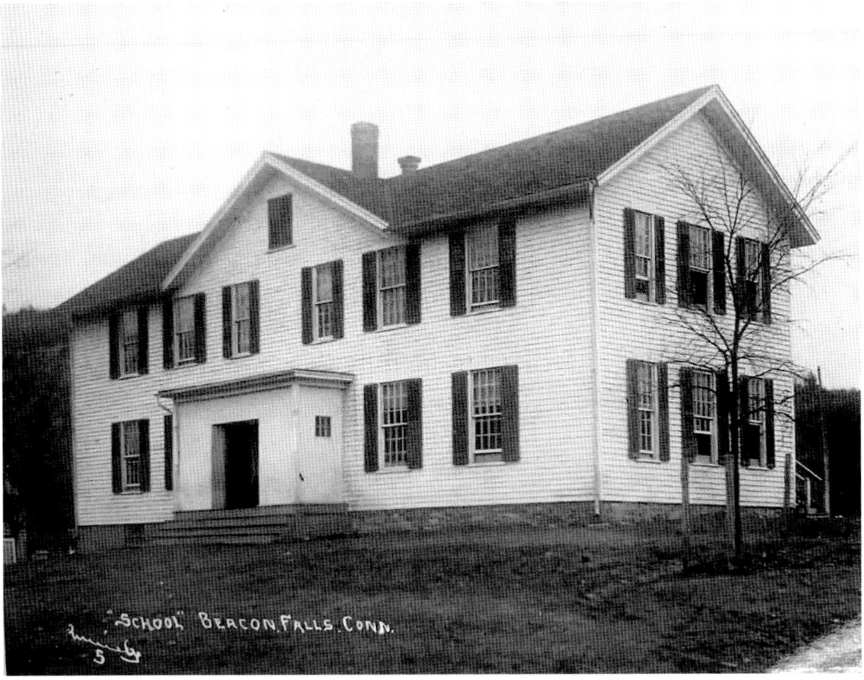

Photo of Center School, which was located on College Avenue. The street was renamed Burton Road around the 1920s. *Courtesy of the Beacon Falls Historical Society.*

The Beacon Falls Public Library

The public library in Beacon Falls can be labeled as having two histories. The townspeople organized to form a library association in November 1922 with the assistance of the State Library Commission. People living in Beacon Falls and Naugatuck together collect nearly one thousand books for the startup library. A room in the Center School was designated as the location of the library, with Miss Daisy Rogers hired as the first librarian.

The library was opened to the public in January 1923. It was quite popular, and since it was decided that the public would be allowed to peruse the book shelves without "staff" help, at the end of the day the library personnel took several hours to straighten the bookshelves back into their Dewey Decimal System order. Library records at the time identified that ninety-one books were loaned on the first day it was open.

In 1951, with enrollment increasing throughout the three schools, the school board made a decision that the room being used for the library was needed as classroom space. The library association made a request of the town to have the Rimmon one-room schoolhouse moved next to the town hall (then still on Main Street), to be used as a library. This request was denied, and as a result, when the school year ended in 1953, the association was disbanded and the library was closed. As it turned out, the Rimmon Schoolhouse was used to warehouse all the library books for the next six years.

In 1957, the library was reborn. Once Laurel Ledge opened with all the town's schoolchildren (K-8th grade) attending there, all the previous schools were abandoned. Around 1955, the town hall was relocated into Center School. The top floor of the building was identified as a possible location for a new public library. Refurbished with shelving and furniture, the library was reopened to the public in April 1959, open for ten hours each week. The library expanded across the hall in 1961, and the facility was open for thirteen hours every week.

The Beacon Falls Public Library remains today as it was more than sixty years ago; it is known as one of the smallest libraries, if not the smallest, in the state of Connecticut.

THE BRONSON COMPANY

In 1882, after the Coe Tannery closed, John Coe and John T. Bronson came to an agreement to exchange properties. The Bronson Company, established in 1839, manufactured brass novelty/ornamental plaques, also called "art goods." The company was in Waterbury, Connecticut. The agreement entailed each site switching locations, which brought the Bronson Company to Beacon Falls and sent the Coe Tannery to Waterbury.

John Bronson found that the Beacon Falls buildings were not completely compatible to the brass novelty business, and he added several new buildings of wood construction to the site. About two years after the move to Beacon Falls, John Bronson retired, and his three sons, Homer, George and Luther Bronson, took over the business. The name was then changed to the Homer D. Bronson Company.

Along with the name change in 1886, the business expanded to manufacturing bronze piano panels, along with the "art goods" in brass and copper. The company also made long or continuous hinges such as those found on pianos. The company was perfectly positioned when automobiles replaced carriages, again making specialty hinges.

In 1895, another wood building was erected that included a water tower, like the towers on the Mill Complex. Unfortunately, the Bronson Company suffered a massive fire in 1899 that destroyed the entire complex of buildings, as they were made of wood. The company rebuilt a one-story brick building on the original site and a two-story office structure closest to South Main Street. These buildings remain to this day.

The Bronson family sold the entire brass manufacturing business in 1910 to a group of Naugatuck Valley businessmen. The name Homer D. Bronson continued until the Beacon Falls factory closed and moved its facilities to Winsted, Connecticut.

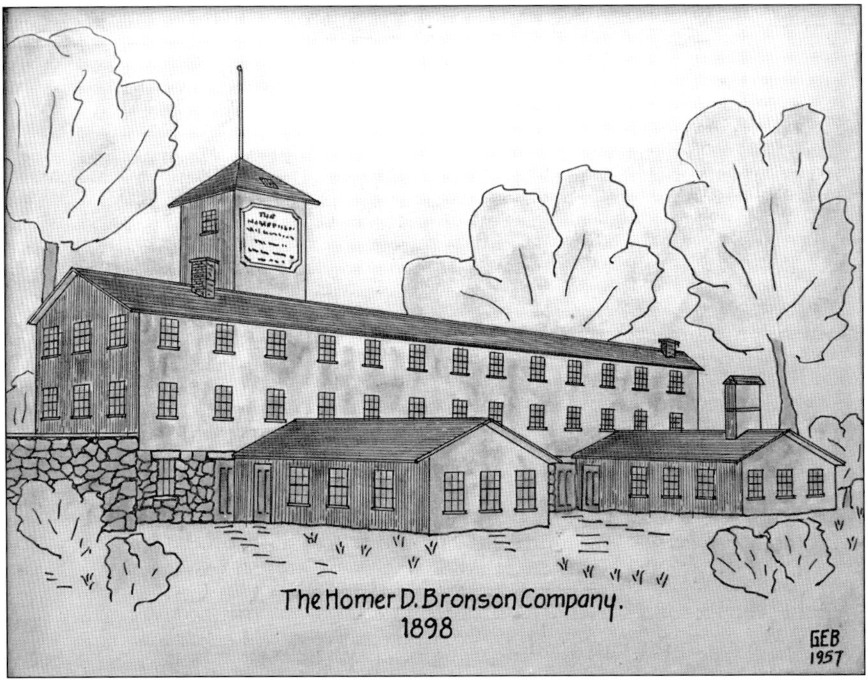

Hand drawing by George Bronson of the Bronson Company building as it looked in 1898. *Courtesy of the Beacon Falls Historical Society.*

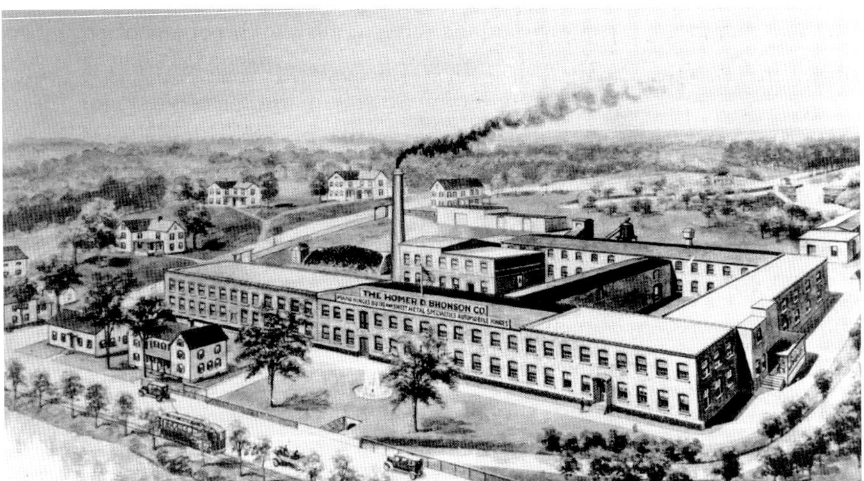

Concept illustration of the Homer D. Bronson Factory Complex, circa 1930. *Courtesy of the Beacon Falls Historical Society.*

BEACON FALLS RUBBER SHOE COMPANY

The Beacon Falls Rubber Shoe Company was unique in the rubber and textile industry. Incorporated in 1898, it grew and prospered over a twenty-two-year period under the guidance of George and his son, Tracy Lewis. The company began modestly, with several hundred employees, and grew its workforce to more than two thousand.

The town of Beacon Falls was the real recipient of this growth. Between 1900 and 1914, Main Street saw the addition and expansion of several businesses, including the Fulton Market and Hoffstadt Drug Store, which became the J.J. O'Connell Drug Store and later H.W. Wilcox Patent Medicines.

Several boardinghouses and hotels were also built. The "hill" area that was part of the Mill Complex saw dozens of homes built because of the Rubber Shoe Company's expansion and prosperity.

In addition to the businesses that grew and prospered due to the rubber company, the company started the Beacon Falls Fire Department and had its own band, which played music during the summer months in the gazebo in the Town Park, which was located where the current firehouse is built.

The images here show an employment marketing advertisement sent to prospective employees. It details how progressive the Beacon Falls Rubber Shoe Company was and the many reasons why someone should consider it for employment.

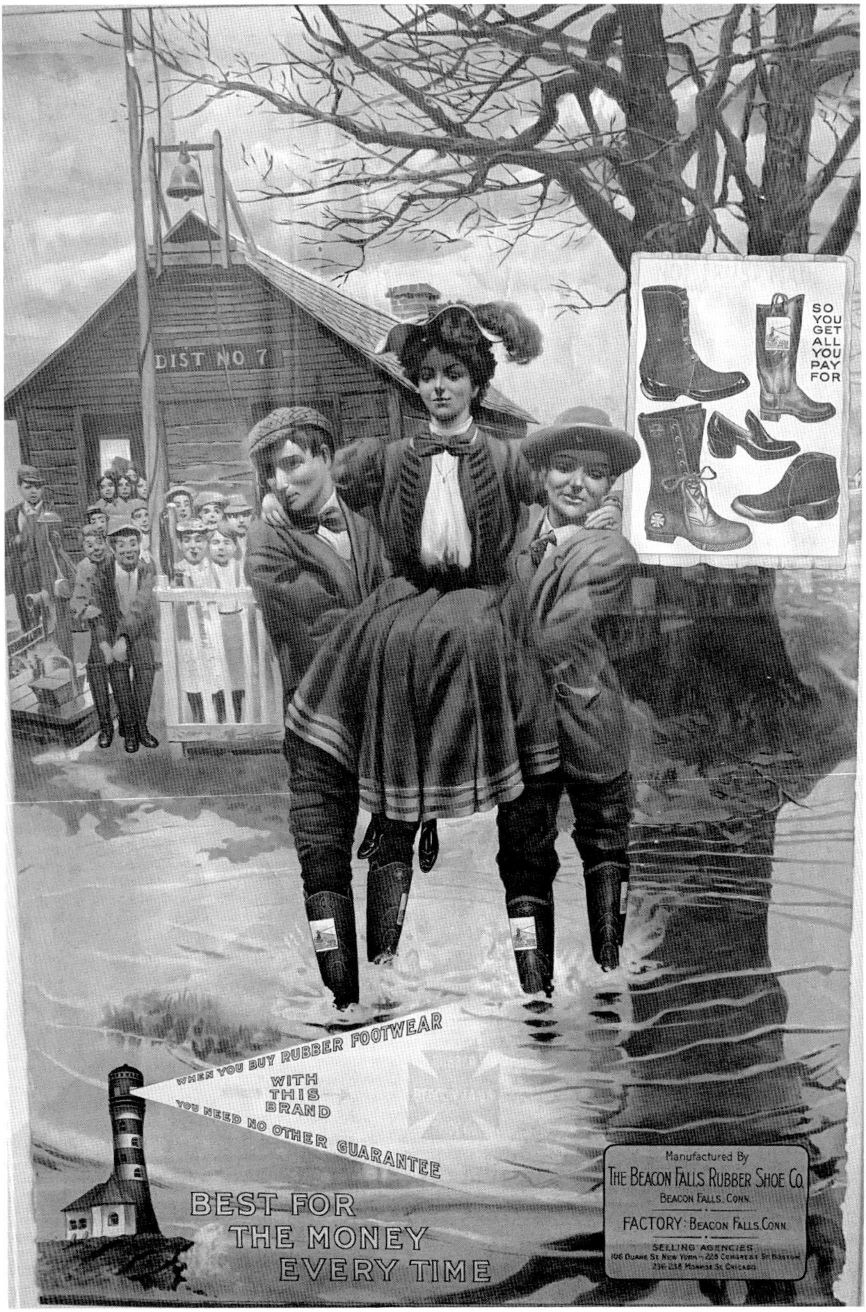

Poster advertisement for the Beacon Falls Rubber Shoe Company. *Courtesy of the Beacon Falls Historical Society.*

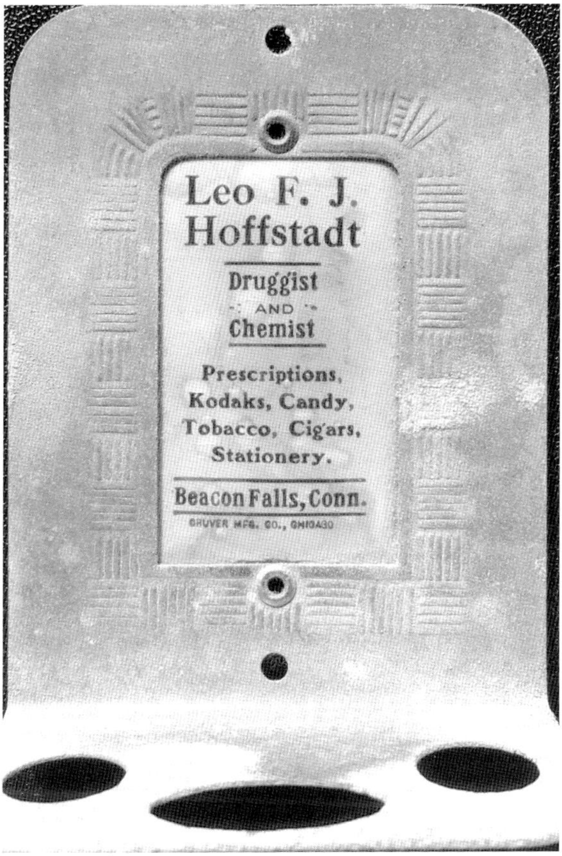

Left: Toothbrush holder from Beacon Falls first drugstore, Hoffstadt's, circa 1905. *Author's collection.*

Below: Homes and "ten-tenement complex" under construction on Highland Avenue, circa 1920s. *Author's collection.*

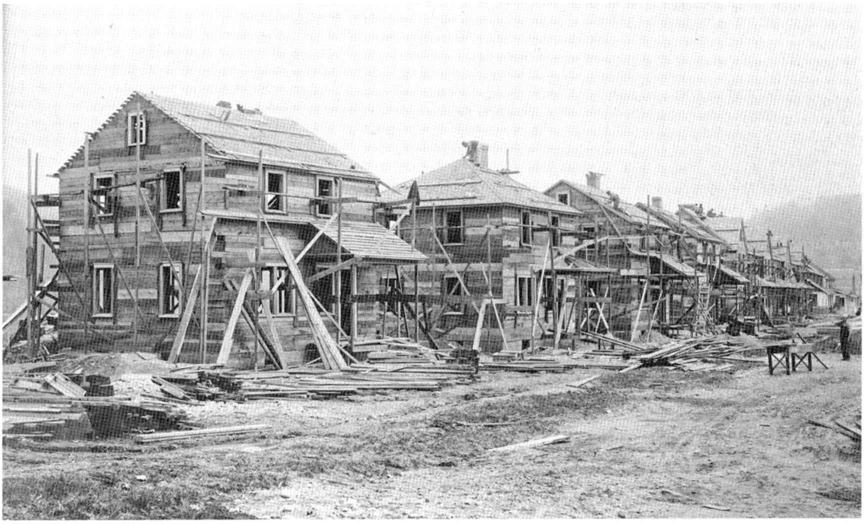

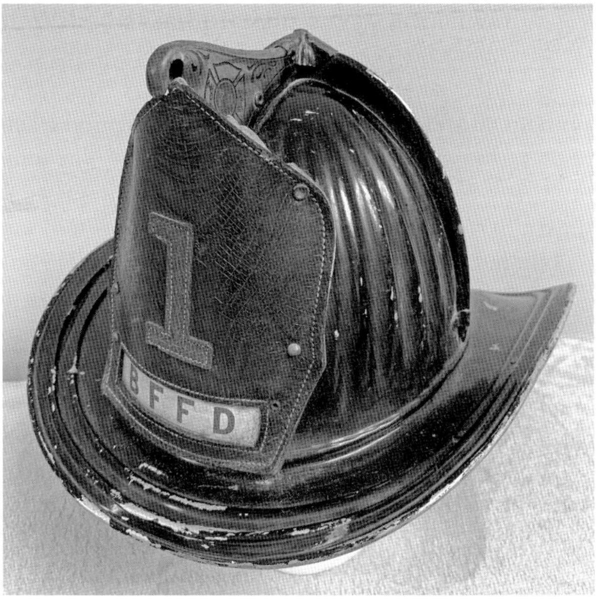

Right: Early Beacon Falls Fire Department helmet. *Author's collection.*

Opposite: Beacon Falls Rubber Shoe Company employment letter marketing brochure. *Author's collection.*

Speech to Employees circa 1945

The following history of the Beacon Falls Rubber Shoe Company was written by an unknown author, assumed to be someone in the company, which at the time was the U.S. Rubber Company. The document, dated circa 1945, appears to have been published for the employees of the company and was given in the form of a speech during a company meeting or perhaps a convention of the sales and marketing team. (Author's note: Several explanations have been added within the speech where clarity was needed.)

Although you have all been connected with the Company for a number of years, you probably are not familiar with all its early activities. We have, therefore, written up a brief history which we thought would be interesting, and acquaint you with the happenings and changes during the forty-five years that we have been operating.

We have been asked many times why the Beacon Falls Rubber Shoe Company happened to be so named.

The Town of Beacon Falls, located in one of the most picturesque spots in New England, was made up of portions of the Towns of Bethany, Seymour, Naugatuck, and Oxford and was incorporated in 1871. It was so named

TRACY S. LEWIS, PRES. & TREAS.
ARTHUR H. DAYTON, VICE PRES.
RICHARD L. FISHER, GEN'L MANAGER
LEWIS C WARNER, VICE PRES. & SEC'Y
EDWARD S. ANDREWS, ASS'T TREAS.
C. E. LITTLE, GEN'L SALES MANAGER

PLEASE ADDRESS ALL COMMUNICATIONS TO THE COMPANY.

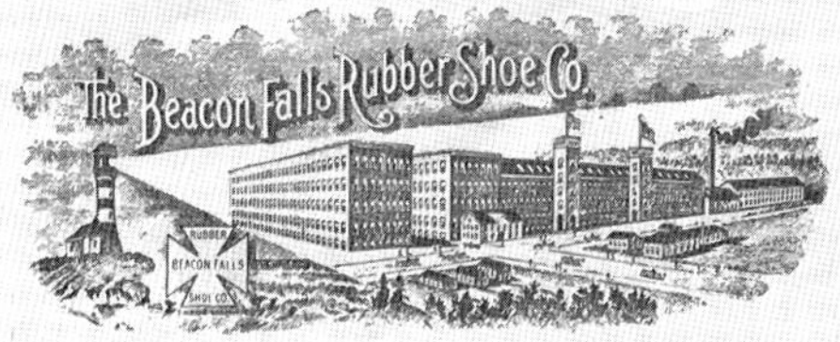

FACTORY
BEACON FALLS, CONN.

SELLING AGENCIES
NEW YORK, 106 DUANE ST.
BOSTON, 241 CONGRESS ST.
CHICAGO, 208-10-12 SO. JEFFERSON ST.
MINNEAPOLIS, 311-15 1ST AVE., NORTH
KANSAS CITY, 926-8 BROADWAY
SAN FRANCISCO, 630-2 HOWARD ST.

EMPLOYMENT DEPARTMENT

Beacon Falls, Conn.

We have written you once before in regard to the matter of coming to Beacon Falls, Conn. to work and if you are still considering our offer or have decided not to come we wish that you would let us know.

We have stated our proposition squarely and honestly. We will pay girls who wish to learn the profitable trade of making rubber shoes $12 a week while learning, which takes from four to six weeks, and furnish them with good board and room at Top Notch Inn, a girls' hotel, at $6.00 a week, which is less than cost to us. After learning girls go on piece work and earn $14, $16, $18 and $20 a week - some even more - working on an average of seven and a half hours a day. The work is not hard and there are real opportunities for advancement.

The kind of women and girls we want are the intelligent, dependable, ambitious kind -- those who are satisfied to live in a small town near large cities -- those who appreciate working for a company which is doing everything within its power to make life enjoyable and worth while for its employees. The work is profitable and steady -- the company has grown so fast that it has been necessary to get workers from outside to come here and live.

Within this folder are more scenes taken about Beacon Falls which should interest you if you are still considering our proposition. Now is the time to decide whether you want this chance to live healthily and happily where you have the advantages of both city and country and the assurance of steady work, year in and year out -- or whether it is for your best interests to remain where you are. In any event we wish that you would write us.

Yours very truly,

BEACON FALLS RUBBER SHOE CO.

William F. Kehoe

Employment Department.

from Beacon Hill, which was within the town limits, and from which a small but beautiful waterfall descended.

In 1863, before the town's incorporation, a three and one-half story brick building was erected, and the manufacture of hard rubber was started by the American Hard Rubber Company. It continued until 1860 when the

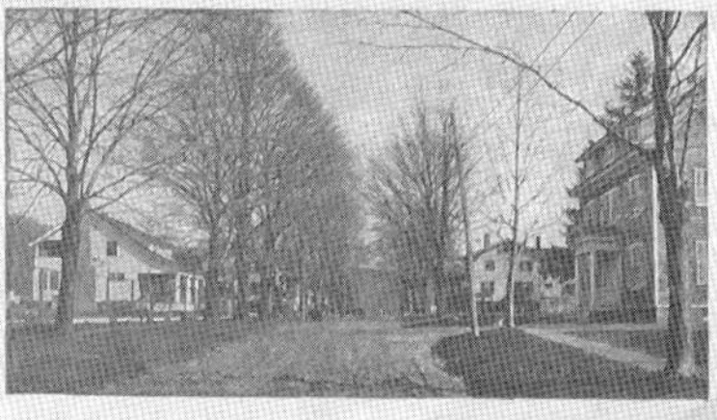

A STREET ON THE HILL

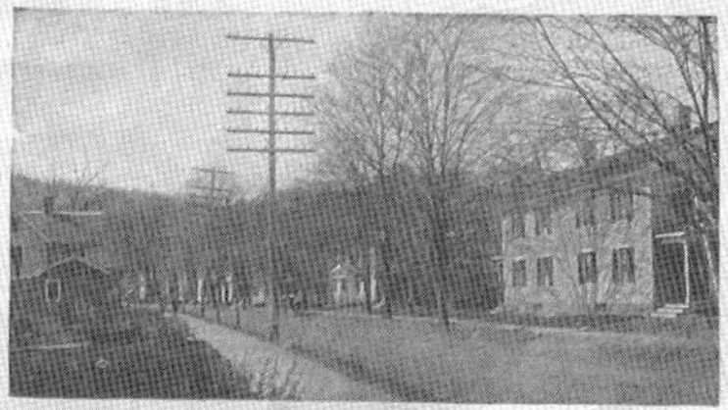

SCENE NEAR THE FACTORY

THERE are some big questions which confront almost every woman and girl who is earning her own living. Three of these questions are:

Is there steady employment, at good wages, ahead of me?

Is it best for me to remain where I am, or live under more healthful living and working conditions in an interesting small town?

Is there an opportunity for me to earn $14, $16, $18 or $20 a week where I am now?

These are the things that we offer the right kind of women and girls at Beacon Falls, Conn. And by the right kind we mean the intelligent, industrious, ambitious kind that are willing to give good service for good pay—the kind that will appreciate the woods and fields and the good times that go with small town life.

Beacon Falls, Conn., is a good town to live in. You can be happy there. You can save money and amount to something. You can have more real friends and better times than you can have working or living in ninety cities out of a hundred.

This might not be so if it were not for the great interest that the Beacon Falls Rubber Shoe Company takes in the welfare of its employees. It pushes ambitious workers ahead rapidly. It offers a bonus for six full days' work. It has provided a fine theatre, athletic field and recreation grounds, a fine hall for dancing and a first-class boarding and rooming hotel—Top Notch Inn—for girls.

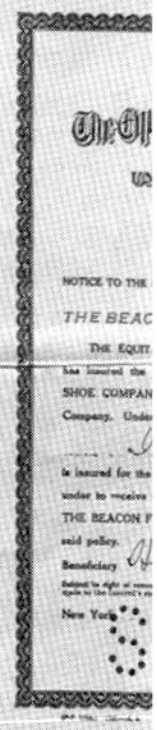

FRE

It has fostered and helped a fine band, a crack basketball team, a girls' club, dancing class, cooking class and bowling teams. It has established a free emergency hospital at the factory. It pays a welfare worker to help the girls get acquainted and enjoy life. It furnishes $500 free life insurance after an employee has been in the service of the company three months.

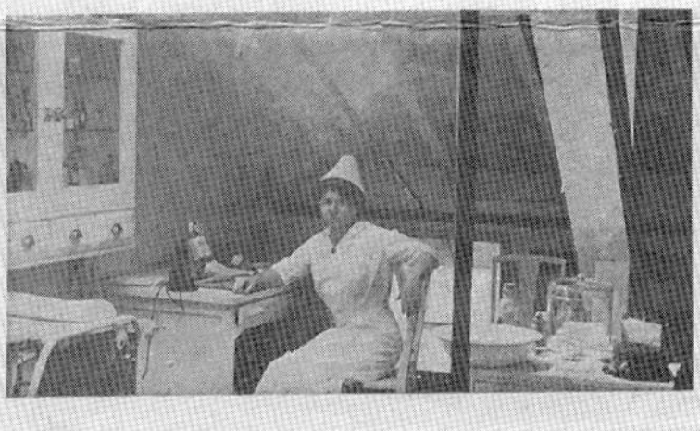

FREE EMERGENCY HOSPITAL

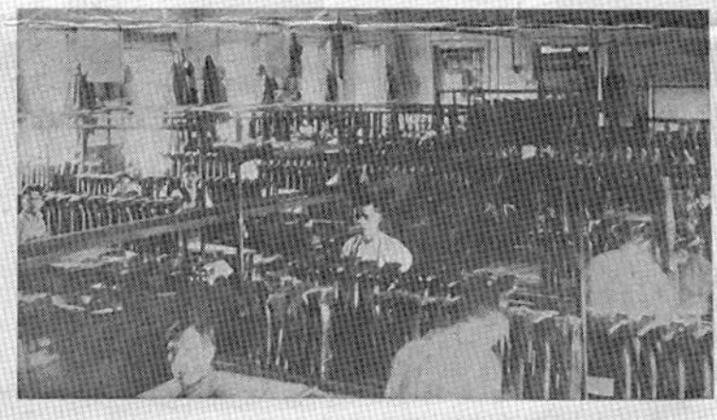

MAKING RUBBER BOOTS

Page two of the employment letter. *Author's collection.*

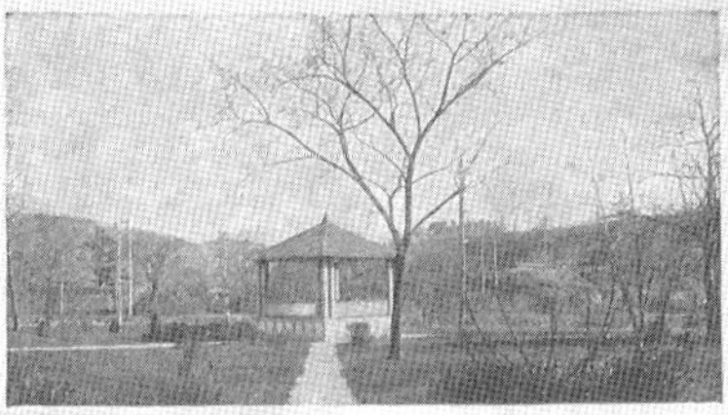

THE PARK AND BANDSTAND

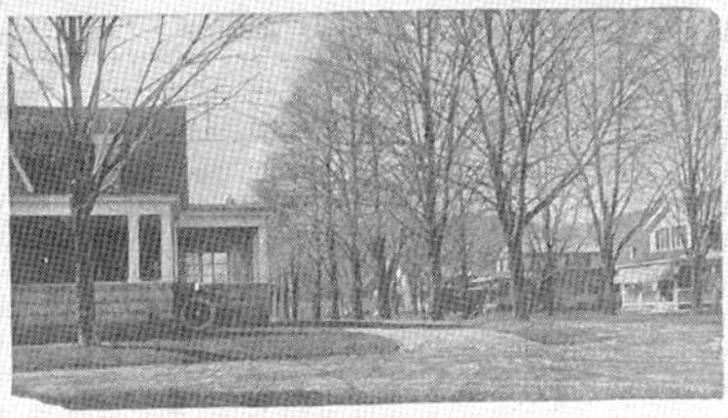

ANOTHER ATTRACTIVE STREET

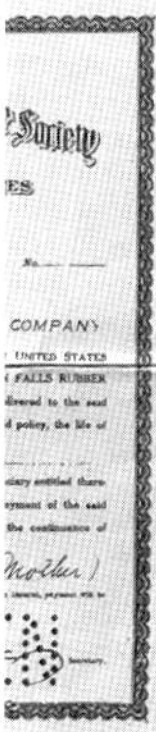

It increases this insurance to $750 after 2½ years of service and to $1,000 after five years.

It enables employees to rent or buy homes at the lowest price and easiest possible terms. It is building attractive cottages to rent or sell to its employees. They can have their own yards and gardens. They can have real neighborhood life. They can live where there is beautiful scenery all about them — fine walks and drives and river rambles.

And then, if they wish, it is only a short trolley ride to nearby cities and the attractions they have to offer, or to New Haven and Savin Rock, the largest seashore resort in the state.

The work is steady, remunerative and not dangerous. The factory is splendidly lighted and ventilated. Competent instructors assist beginners so that at the end of a month they can become skilled workers, if they are intelligent and wish to advance. Already we employ practically all the women and girl workers who live in Beacon Falls and the neighboring towns and our business is growing so fast that we must have 100 more girls this year.

As examples of what some girls are earning—two girls, Mildred and June Castle, who have not been long at Beacon Falls, are each earning $24 per week, while others, like Henrietta Burnham, Geneva Stott, Grace Snooks and Louise Byrne, are earning $20, $18 and $17 per week.

In this folder we present some views taken at Beacon Falls — also an illustration of the free life insurance policy we give to our employees — a policy in The Equitable Life Assurance Society, one of the strongest and best companies in the life insurance field.

Consider well if the things we have told you about are not the things that you wish in life. This is an exceptional opportunity for you to choose a good place to work and live—a place where every industrious man and woman can be happy and prosperous if they wish to be.

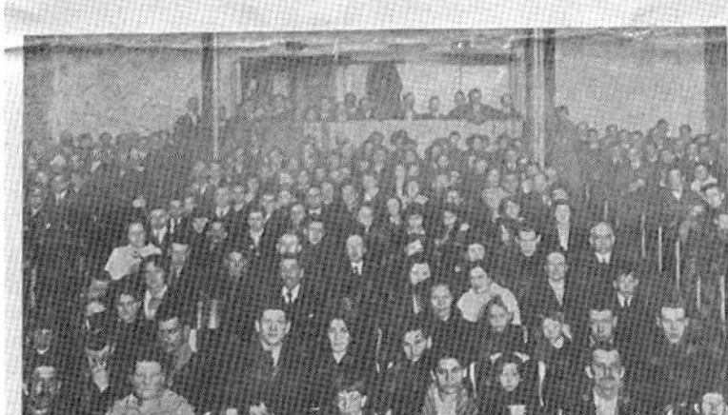

AT THE PICTURE SHOW

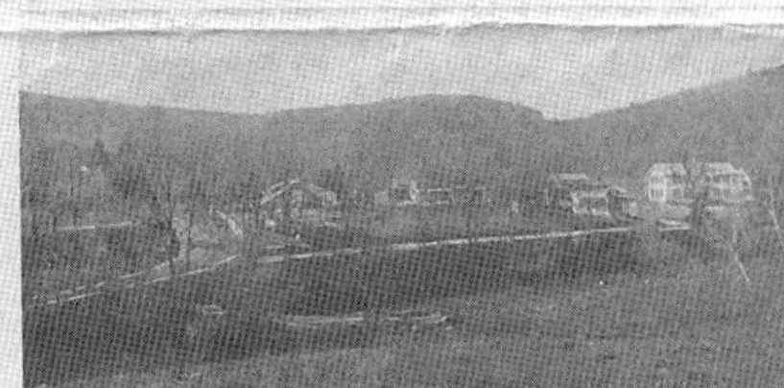

A BEACON FALLS SCENE

Page three of the employment letter. *Author's collection.*

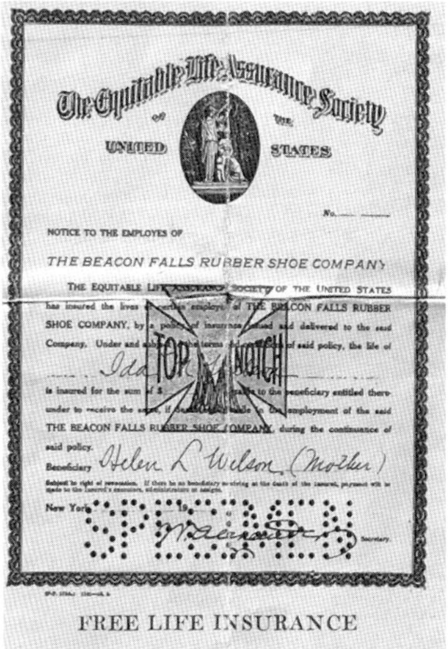
The Equitable Life Assurance Society of the United States

No.

NOTICE TO THE EMPLOYES OF

THE BEACON FALLS RUBBER SHOE COMPANY

THE EQUITABLE LIFE ASSURANCE SOCIETY OF THE UNITED STATES has insured the lives [illegible] employes of THE BEACON FALLS RUBBER SHOE COMPANY, by a policy of insurance [illegible] and delivered to the said Company. Under and subject to the terms [illegible] of said policy, the life of

Ida [illegible]

is insured for the sum of $ [illegible] to the beneficiary entitled thereunder to receive the same, if [illegible] in the employment of the said THE BEACON FALLS RUBBER SHOE COMPANY, during the continuance of said policy.

Beneficiary Helen L. Wilson (Mother)

New York [illegible] 19

Secretary.

SPECIMEN

FREE LIFE INSURANCE

An example of an employee insurance agreement. BFRSC provided insurance to all its employees. *Author's collection.*

business was moved to College Point, Long Island, New York.

The building remained idle until 1863, at which time it was purchased by the Home Woolen Company. It was used for the manufacture of woolen cloth and shawls. The Company was prosperous, and in 1867 erected another building, the same size as the original building, thereby doubling their capacity. The two buildings mentioned are the ones on main street with the elevator towers in front.

The expenditure, up to this time, for building and equipment, amounted to a half million dollars which was a sizable amount for those times.

The manufacture of woolen goods was carried on from 1863 for many years. During that time several different companies operated the plant and, between the changes, the buildings and machinery would be idle for some time. It is interesting to note here that the Company that owned and operated the mill also owned practically all the real estate in town. [*NOTE: Throughout the early history of the mill up to circa 1916, the nearly one hundred acres of property that is the "hill" section today comprising Wolfe, Maple, Century, Highland, North and South Circle were part of the mill property.*]

For several years after the last woolen company [*the Standard Woolen Company*] had ceased to operate, the town was like a deserted village. The property at this time was owned by the Beacon Mill & Power Company until 1898 when the Beacon Falls Rubber Shoe Company was incorporated and purchased all the factory buildings and real estate. Mr. George A. Lewis, son of Samuel J. Lewis, founder of the Goodyear Metallic Rubber Shoe Company at Naugatuck and later President of the Wales Goodyear Company with whom he had been associated for over thirty years, was the President of this new venture in Beacon Falls. Associated with him were a number of men who had been with him at Naugatuck—Mr. Adna Warner who afterwards went to the Mishawaka Rubber Company, Mr. L.C. Warner who was Superintendent of the Beacon Falls Rubber Shoe Company for many years, and Mr. Lewis' son Tracy S. Lewis.

For Those Who Want Real Home Life in a Healthy, Live Town, with Good Wages, Steady Employment and Plenty of Enjoyment

We are willing to go more than half way to meet you and give you an opportunity to see just what this opportunity at Beacon Falls means. If you are interested and do not live too far away, we will send our woman welfare worker to see you—to tell you about the company, the work, the town and the people who live in it.

There are good schools and churches here, both Catholic and Protestant. The railroad, the trolley road and the Naugatuck River run right through the town. There are three changes of bill weekly at the Top Notch Theatre. There are frequent dances of a most enjoyable sort.

If you wish to come here we will give you good board and room at Top Notch Inn at $6 a week, which is less than it costs the company. This girls' hotel is an ideal home, but girls may live elsewhere if they prefer to. As we have told you previously, the clean, neat rooms at Top Notch Inn are lighted by electricity and there are plenty of good white enameled baths and other conveniences, including stationary tubs, with hot and cold running water, which the girls can use for washing their own clothes if they desire to do so. There is a fine recreation room at the Inn.

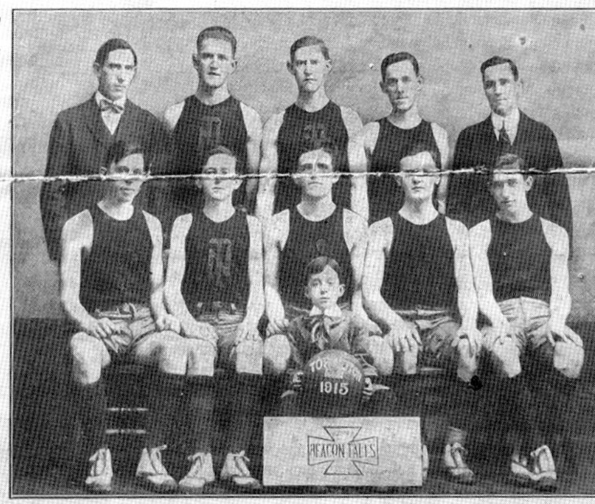

TOP NOTCH BASKETBALL TEAM

We know that you will like it here once you have become acquainted with the work and have made some friends. Just give the opportunity your fullest consideration and write us to-day—as this is the last time we shall address you upon the subject. We have done our best to tell you truthfully and honestly about the things in which we believe you would be most interested. We will do our best to help and advance you if you come, so that you may wish to live in Beacon Falls for the rest of your life. We'll meet you at the train if notified ahead and refund your fare here after you have worked for us 3 months.

Address

BEACON FALLS RUBBER SHOE COMPANY
BEACON FALLS, CONN.
Employment Department

Page four of the employment letter. *Author's collection.*

The company was successful from the start and as production was increased additional buildings were erected from 1899 to 1919. The building you are now in was the original office building and was located across the street.

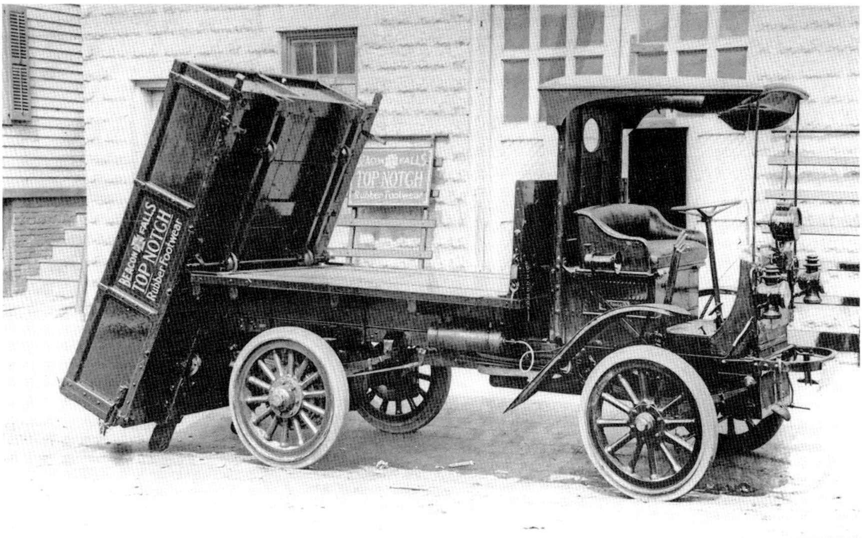

Circa 1910 dump truck that was part of the BFRSC fleet of trucks. *Author's collection.*

A large portion of the power for the plant was derived by water from the Naugatuck River, supplemented by steam power. This was before the days of direct electric drives.

The first ticket of shoes was made on March 15, 1899. By ticket we might mention that a ticket was made up in the office showing the kinds of shoes, sizes and quantity that were to be made on a specific date, about a week hence. A copy was sent to all departments so the stock could be mixed, run, cut and assembled in the making room on the making date. The out-of-town employees came by train as there were no trolleys in the early days of the company.

The first ticket was for 144 pairs, a small beginning, which grew to five and a half million pairs in the year 1920, which including the production at College Point (Long Island). [*Note: The College Point factory is mentioned further along in this notice to the company.*]

The original branches [of the company] were at Boston, New York and Chicago. The Boston branch was operated by Mark Converse who afterwards formed and became the President of the Converse Rubber Shoe Company. Other branches were opened later at Minneapolis, Kansas City and Pittsburgh. The Kansas City branch would later move to St Louis.

President George Lewis passed away in 1914 and his son, Tracy S. Lewis succeeded him.

About 1911 Major Fisk, who had been in the Philippines with the U.S. Constabulary force, became associated with the Company as Assistant Superintendent. He was very much interested in fiber or rope soled shoes, and started experimenting with them. A Company was formed named "Fisole Company," the officers and directors being members of the Beacon Falls organization. A quantity of these rope sole shoes were made and distributed over the United States by the regular salesmen. A large quantity was also sold to the U.S. government for use in the Philippines.

During the first world war [World War I], the labor situation in the Naugatuck Valley became very acute, due to the proximity of Bridgeport, Waterbury, and New Haven, where all labor possible was devoted to making war materials. As we were making a quantity of rubber footwear for the government, we could not spare enough labor to manufacture canvas footwear, so another factory was started at College Point, Long Island. Here our production reached a maximum of one and a half million pairs of canvas a year, and one year we made over 700,000 pairs of light gum shoes.

In the early years of the Company, the canvas footwear line consisted of black, white, and brown oxfords with a black sole. The sales amounted to a few hundred cases a year and they were made for us by the Maynard Shoe Company at Maynard NH. It was, therefore, a long jump from that beginning to our 1922 College Point production of one and a half million pairs, and, in later years, this was greatly increased at Beacon Falls.

To reduce expenses and bring the manufacturing under one roof again, College Point was closed and in 1926 the equipment was moved to Beacon Falls.

In 1921 the President, Tracy S. Lewis died and the Company was taken over by the U.S. Rubber Company. At this time the U.S. Rubber was a heavy

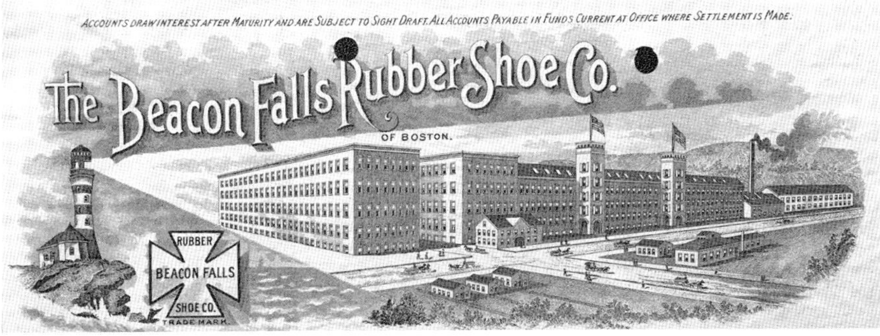

BFRSC letterhead. Typical of its kind, the image overstates the actual factory buildings that existed, circa 1900. *Author's collection.*

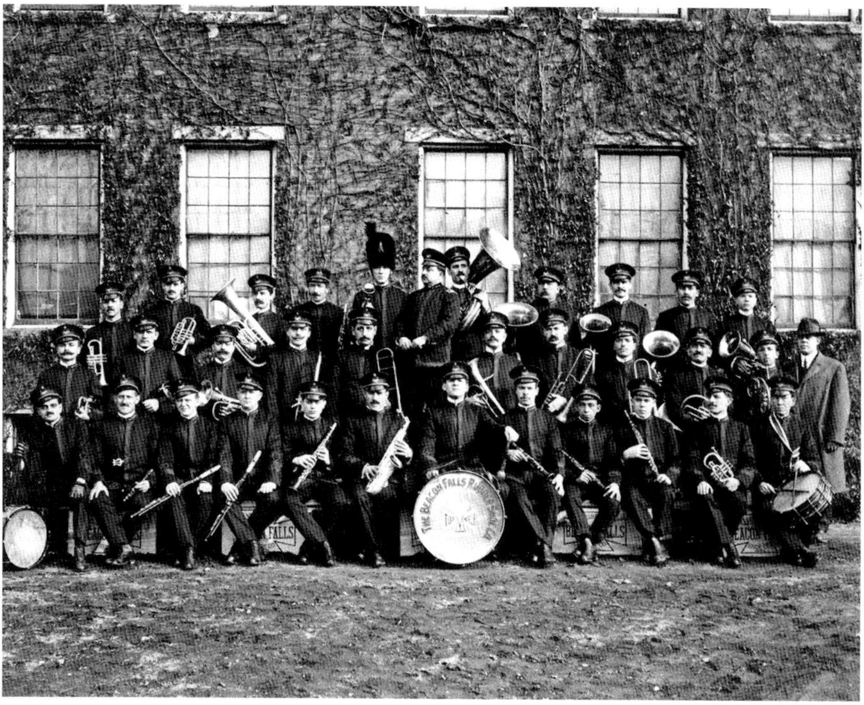

BFRSC Band, which entertained employees in the park during the summer months. *Author's collection.*

stockholder in Beacon Falls and besides protecting their own interests they didn't want to have a failure in the rubber business at that critical time or have the plant get in the hands of unscrupulous competitors. Three men from the U.S. Rubber Company were transferred to Beacon Falls to operate the plant, namely Frank E. Church, President, Fred W. Strong, Treasurer, and Henry C. Wagner, Factory Manager.

After a few years Mr. Church was transferred to the New York Office as General Sales Manager, and Mr. Strong was also transferred to New York as Branch Manager, which position he still holds. C.E. Little, now of Servus Rubber Company, followed Mr. Church as President of Beacon Falls.

Manufacturing was continued at Beacon Falls until 1930 when all manufacturing activities were transferred to the Naugatuck factories.

Mr. W.F. Cairns was placed in charge of Beacon Falls in 1931. He continued as General Manager until 1943 when he was transferred to Mishawaka as General Manager of the Clothing Division and was seceded at Beacon Falls by C.F. Kadlee. [*NOTE: The remaining text from the speech that follows*

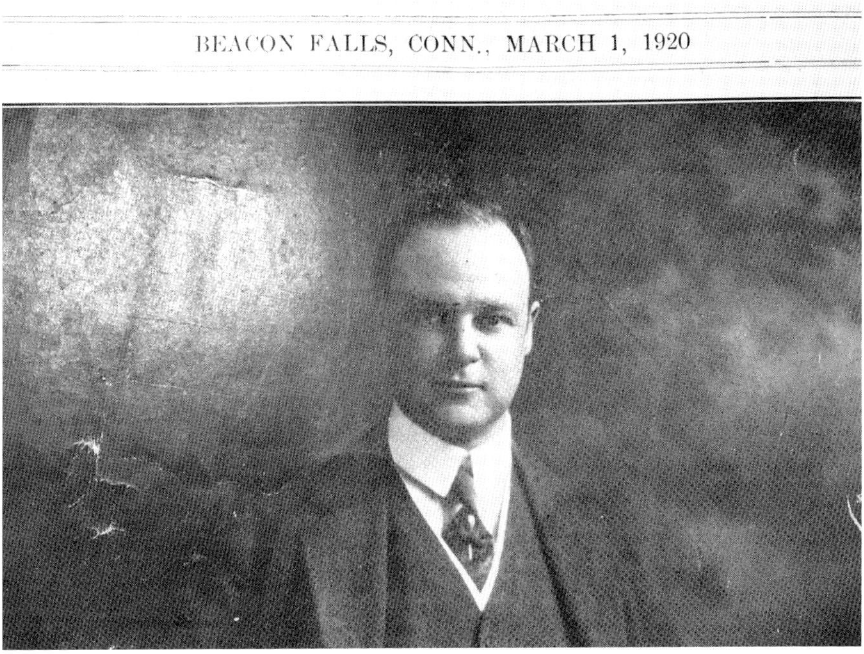

Mr. Tracy S. Lewis, 1920. Lewis would die unexpectedly one year later, in April 1921. *Author's collection.*

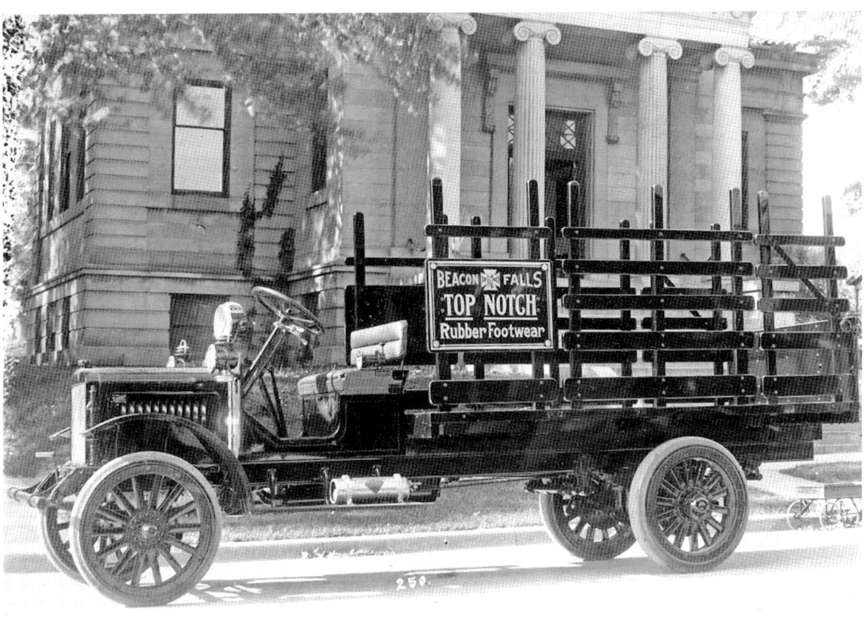

BFRSC delivery truck. *Author's collection.*

is most interesting, as it identifies several other rubber companies, some of which were competitors, that were started or whose management included former Beacon Falls Rubber Shoe Company employees. This implies that the Beacon Falls Rubber Shoe Company was a large influence in the rubber shoe industry during the early twentieth century.]

Another concern in which Beacon Falls was interested was the Medford Woolen Company of Massachusetts, who were manufacturers of felt boots. This was an old-time company in which President G.A. Lewis was interested and held the office of President. It ran as a separate company for a number of years, and in the early years of the Beacon Falls Rubber Shoe Company it was bought in and wholly owned by them.

Their efforts were devoted to the manufacture of felt boots of which we sold a large quantity in combination with overs. [*Note: It appears that within the company the rubber overshoe products were internally nicknamed "overs."*]

During World War #1 the plant went into the manufacture of socks in large quantities, and this was continued for some time after the war.

When the Beacon Falls Rubber Shoe Company was taken over by the U.S. Rubber Company the Medford plant was disposed of.

You no doubt will be interested in knowing when some of the other rubber footwear companies were started.

Goodyear Rubber, Middletown, CT was started in 1852 using the brand name "Gold Seal" and ran successfully until 1928 when it was reincorporated, and Frank Church, former President of Beacon Falls went in as President. Mr. Church would later take a position at the Hood Rubber Company as its General Manager.

The Tyler Rubber Company was started in 1856 where it manufactured rubber sundries, and in later years it would manufacture rubber footwear.

LaCrosse was started in 1898, the same year that Beacon Falls was organized.

Converse Rubber Company was started in 1908 by Mark Converse, a former manager of the Beacon Falls branch in Boston.

Cambridge Rubber was started in 1915 by Mr. McPherson and was incorporated in 1923.

Endicott Johnson was a large manufacturer of rubber footwear for many years and it was about 1915 that they started to equip a rubber footwear plant.

Servus Rubber Company organized in 1921 and several former Beacon Falls men were prime movers in the formation of the company, among them were Jud Adams, branch manager from Chicago, and John Crowley, former superintendent at College Point and Beacon Falls.

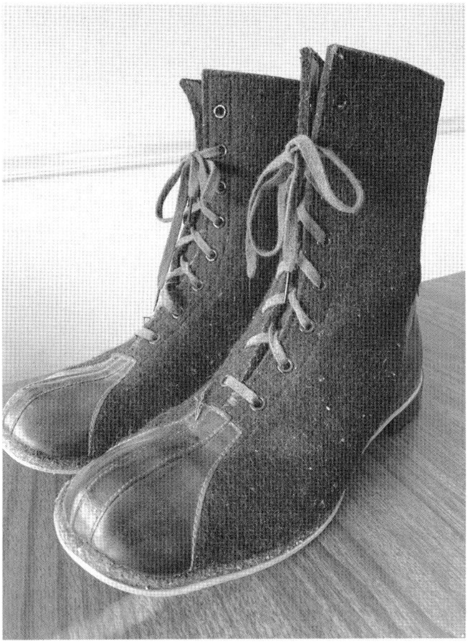

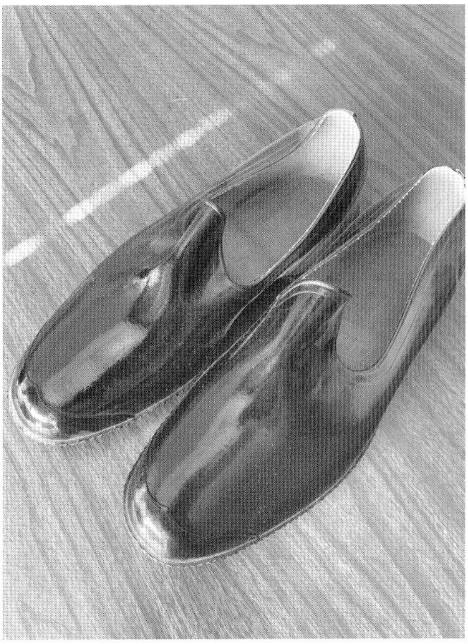

Left: Pair of felt boots manufactured for the BFRSC by the Medford Woolen Company. *Photo by author, author's collection.*

Right: BFRSC men's overshoes or "overs." *Photo by author, author's collection.*

Up to a few years ago we operated under the name, Beacon Falls Rubber Shoe Company, as a separate individual Company. However, it was decided by the parent Company to change the name to Beacon Falls Rubber Footwear, a Division of the U.S. Rubber Company. We are therefore an actual part of the big Company, thereby having the benefit of their vast experience in manufacturing, selling, advertising—in fact everything that goes to make up a successful organization. All this is of a great benefit to us in marketing our product and helps to reduce our cost of operation, making it lower than it would be if we were a small independent company. As yet there are no definite post war plans, but we believe that the present set-up will continue when we return to a peace time basis.

We have not attempted to go into detail in this resume but have hit most of the high spots that happened over a course of forty-four years.

The names of Beacon Falls and Top Notch are still names to be reckoned with among competitors and dealers. We have weathered one world war and several depressions, and, when the present conflict is over, we expect to go forward with renewed energy and keep our name constantly before the public as the brand to tie to.

COMPETITION

THE RUBBER TRUST

In the years leading up to the incorporation of the Beacon Falls Rubber Shoe Company in 1898, there was already a large number of competitors in the rubber industry footwear space. Around 1892, a business financier named Charles Flint joined with eleven such companies in an effort to consolidate and stabilize the rubber footwear market. This new business would be become the United States Rubber Company (aka U.S. Rubber) and would be known as the "Rubber Trust."

Controlling nearly 50 percent of the nation's footwear sales, the Rubber Trust actively pursued other rubber footwear companies in an attempt to merge them into the trust. The Beacon Falls Rubber Shoe Company was a prime target of the trust because of its large market share. The Beacon Falls Rubber Shoe Company actively protected its independence and fought strongly against its much larger rival. The advertisements seen here were just a few of the notices the Beacon Falls company sent to its customers worldwide in its campaign to remain independent—"We are outside the trust."

Upon Tracy S. Lewis's death, the life of the Beacon Falls Rubber Shoe Company as a privately owned business began to unravel. By 1931, U.S. Rubber had acquired the Rubber Shoe Company. It was the beginning of the end of its existence in Beacon Falls.

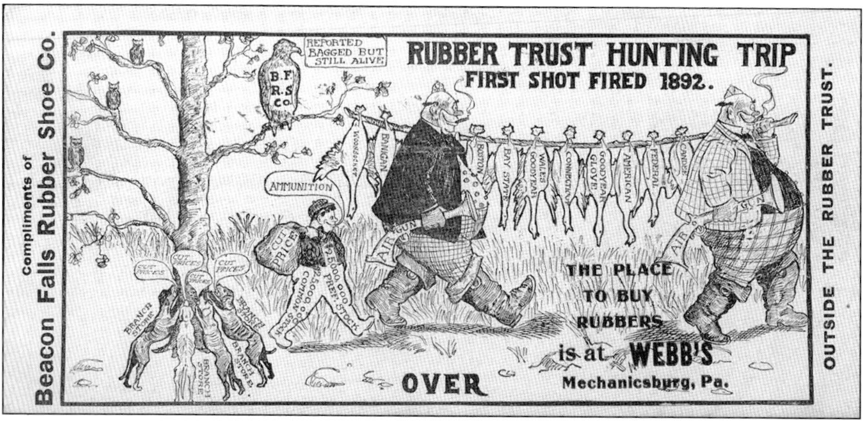

SEE BIRDS on other side; they represent the brands in the so-called RUBBER TRUST. Ask for **BEACON FALLS RUBBERS.** It keeps us outside the Trust.

WE ARE OUTSIDE THE TRUST.

Boston, January 2, 1905.

DON'T BE URGED

INTO PLACING YOUR RUBBER ORDER FOR ANOTHER SEASON 'TILL OUR SALESMAN SEES YOU.

REASONS WHY.

Our goods are unlike other makes, OUR PRICES ARE UNLIKE OTHER MAKES, our lasts enable you to carry fewer styles, sell you direct Hip Boots to Footholds, goods fresh from the factory. Please show your appreciation of our not advancing prices last June by your support in the way of orders. We are really on your side of the fence, can you afford not to help keep us there?

BEACON FALLS RUBBER SHOE CO.,
228 CONGRESS STREET.

Top: BFRSC anti-trust ad card sent to its customers. *Author's collection.*

Middle: Text description of the anti-trust ad card. *Author's collection.*

Bottom: 1905 postcard sent to BFRSC customers from its Boston headquarters. *Author's collection.*

TOP NOTCH LOGO

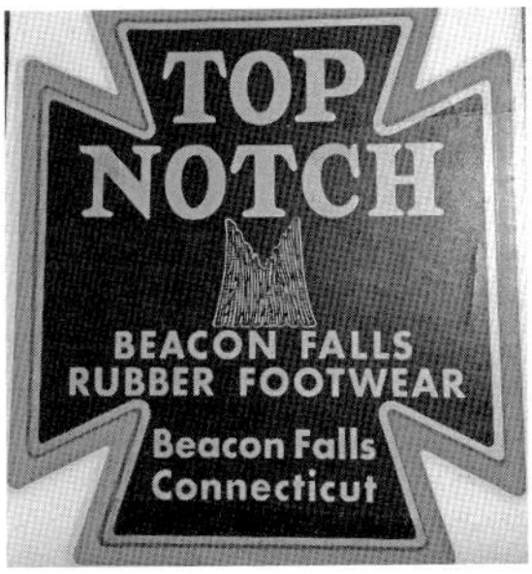

BFRSC's official logo, used on all shipping crates. *Author's collection.*

The company trademark from the beginning was a Maltese cross. Around 1913, when the Top Notch line of shoe was created, the trademark was redesigned to include a "top" and a "notch." Looking at the trademark logo, there is the image of a trunk of a tree with a notch. A top, the type of spinning top that the youth of the early 1900s played with, was added in the center of the notch. Sometime later, a competitor by the name of Top-Top claimed infringement rights, and the top was removed from the logo.

THE TRACY S. LEWIS HOUSE

The Tracy S. Lewis House was purchased by the Town of Beacon Falls in 2008 as the possible site to build a new media center (library). After numerous discussions, including financial considerations, the proposal changed to a multi-use facility that would include a community center. The cost of such a building was never finalized, but it was assumed that such a building was an easier to sell to the taxpayers.

Now, thirteen years later, the buildings, which also included the Carriage House in the rear of the property, are sitting empty and in disrepair. It was determined and voted on by the Board of Selectmen in a split vote (two to one) that the buildings would be destroyed, and a salvager was eventually contracted to remove the very attributes that made the house such a unique building, according to a historical review and assessment study.

The history of the Lewis House has been best represented in the "Tracy Lewis House Conditions Assessment & Reuse Study," created by the Paul Bailey Architect firm; it was commissioned by the Town of Beacon Falls and presented to the town on May 10, 2010. The study was commissioned to assist the Media Center Building Committee in determining if the house was suitable to be used as part of the proposed new facility or if it should be removed to make space for a new building. The study described the house:

> *The Tracy S. Lewis house is a large wood frame residence built in 1916 for a wealthy industrialist and socialite. The house, grounds and entire neighborhood was part of a master plan designed by the renowned landscape*

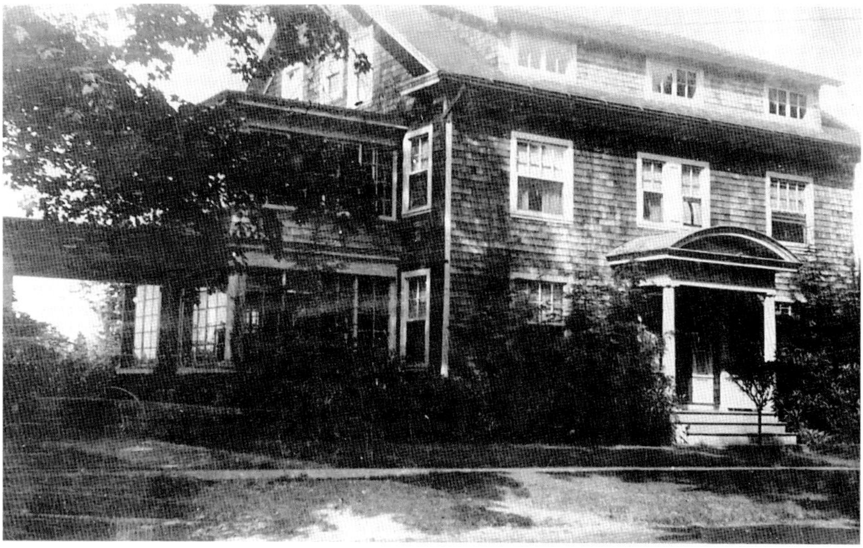

Front view of the Tracy S. Lewis Home, circa 1932. Image comes courtesy of Robert Vernon, who was two years old and living in the Lewis House when the photo was taken.

> *architects, Olmsted Brothers. The property on which the house was built belonged to the Beacon Falls Rubber Shoe Company and had previously belonged to other mills. The history of these manufacturing companies reflects the history of the town and the entire Naugatuck Valley.*

The true origin of the house may date to around the 1860s, and it very well may have been built earlier by the American Hard Rubber Company in the 1850s. This requires further research, but the historian working for the Bailey firm reviewed the structure's foundation and the upper course of bricks and stated that the basement area construction methods were indicative of stone walls from the 1860s to the early twentieth century.

Maps of the mid-1850s and 1860s show two different-shaped houses on this site. It was also noted that several additional houses on Wolfe Avenue have similar construction and that they themselves are dated to the 1860s. All these buildings are shown on the 1968 Beers maps and are the "ten" houses mentioned in several records as being part of the mill properties of this period.

Tracy Lewis is listed in town records of 1903–5 as a town official, and his address was this specific house at 35 Wolfe Avenue. Prior to moving into the home, Lewis lived in what was called the "Lewis Boarding House," which is the large multifamily building next to the Beacon Falls Congregational Church.

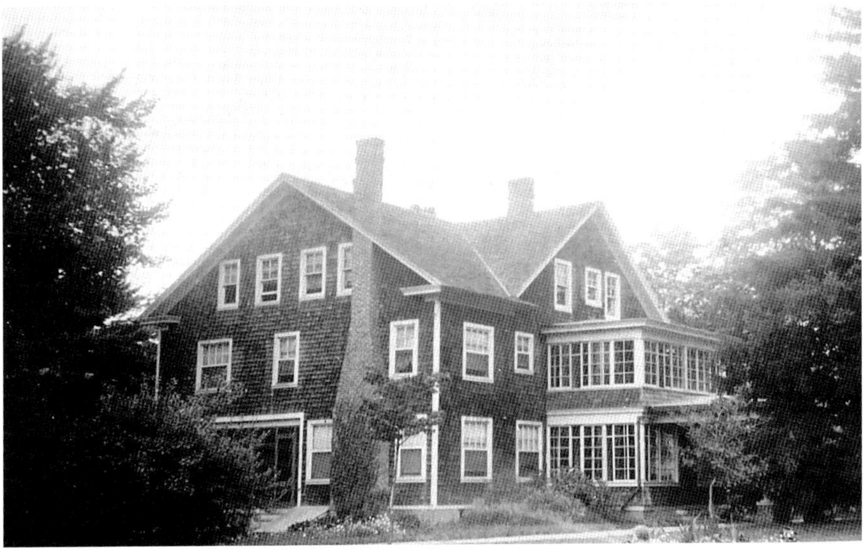

Back view of the Tracy S. Lewis Home, circa 1932. Image comes courtesy of Robert Vernon, who was two years old and living in the Lewis House when the photo was taken.

The Bailey historian further stated:

> *The Tracy S. Lewis House is a rare and intact example of an early 20th century high-end residence. The house was built by Beacon Falls' most prominent citizen and owner of its leading manufacturing company. Built along a residential street overlooking the mill, the house stands as a reminder of the town's industrial founding and growth.*

The reuse study findings concluded:

> *The house is an excellent candidate for further study and preservation. Preservation of the Tracy S. Lewis House would ensure that the stories of Mr. Lewis' life and his role in Beacon Falls continue for future generations. The house's many intact architectural details and features are timeless representations of quality design and planning. Although the house may no longer serve as a residential structure, careful and creative planning should be implemented to allow for adaptive use.*

The Bailey study went further than just evaluating the property for reuse. It defined the areas of concern that would need repair as part of any renovation. In addition, concept plans for building the proposed media/

community center on the full site were created. These included how the house might be incorporated into the design, as well as a second set of drawings should the decision involve the house's removal.

Regardless of the conclusion of the condition assessment, the building committee's ultimately decision was that renovating the house did not fit the perceived plans for the property. The committee added that the "conclusions of the Bailey Study were full of misinformation and inaccuracies," and therefore the study was not relevant to any final decision. Even though the verbal direction given to the building committee by the First Selectman was not to use the cost difference between incorporating the main house in the project versus tearing it down and building a new structure, the building committee indeed stated that difference as a reason to raze the structure.

The Tracy S. Lewis home was listed in the State Register of Historic Places in 2010.

DEPOT STREET BRIDGE

The original "Covered Bridge" (which was then called Bridge Street Bridge) was constructed by the American Hard Rubber Company in 1856 as the replacement to another bridge that was located about three hundred feet south of the current bridge. That first bridge was built in 1835 near the "rock-cut." It was destroyed by a flood in 1855.

In 1892, it was noticed that a sixty-foot section on the eastern end of the bridge was deteriorating to the point that repairs were needed, and a metal structure was built (as shown in the image here).

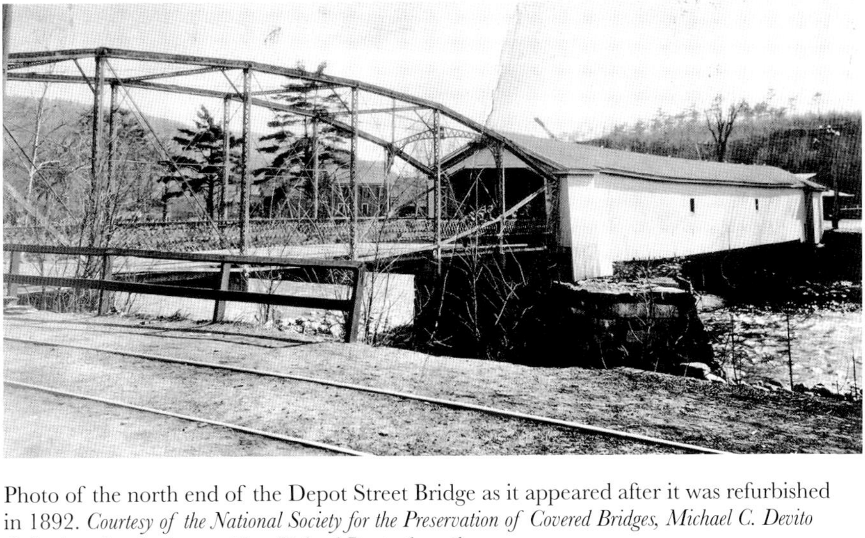

Photo of the north end of the Depot Street Bridge as it appeared after it was refurbished in 1892. *Courtesy of the National Society for the Preservation of Covered Bridges, Michael C. Devito Collection, given by then president Richard Roy to the author.*

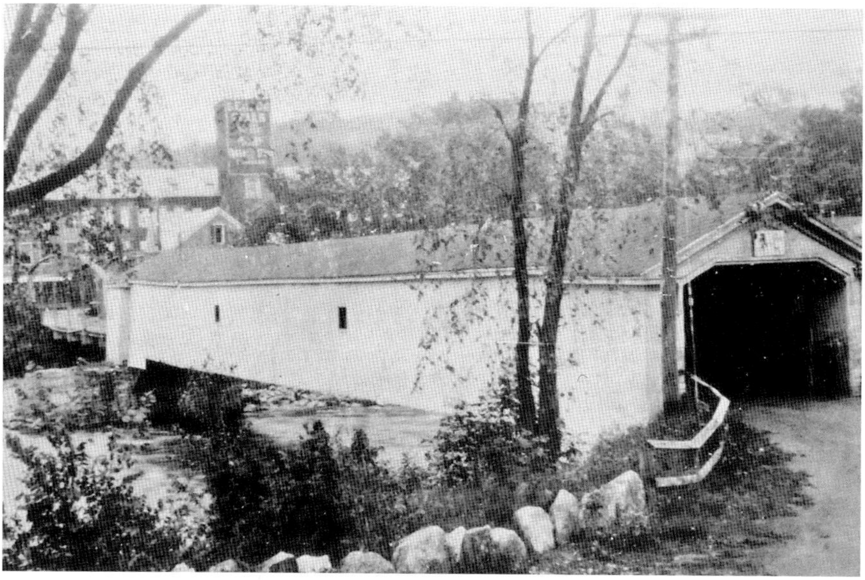

Photo of the south end of the Depot Street Bridge as it appeared after it was refurbished in 1892. *Courtesy of the National Society for the Preservation of Covered Bridges, Michael C. Devito Collection, given by then president Richard Roy to the author.*

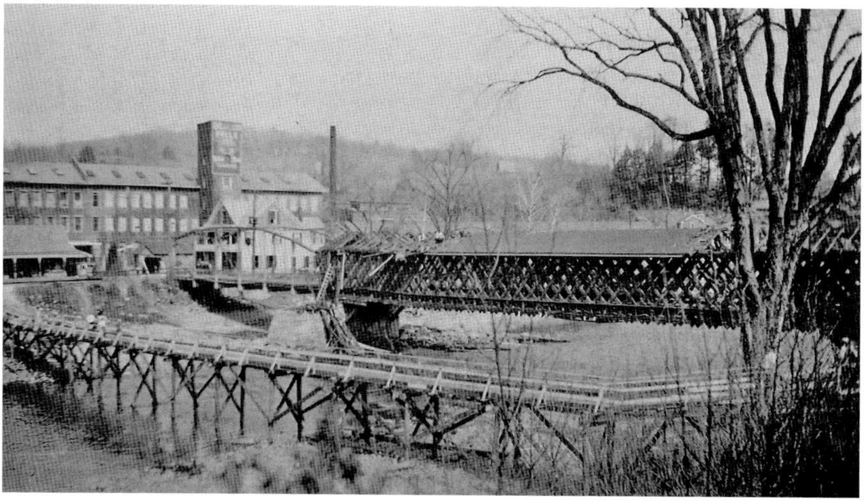

The demolition of the Depot Street Bridge in 1935. *Courtesy of the National Society for the Preservation of Covered Bridges, Michael C. Devito Collection, given by then president Richard Roy to the author.*

In 1934, with the remaining wooden structure rapidly showing its age, the town decided to replace the entire bridge with a state-of-the-art 212-foot-long Parker truss–style metal bridge at a cost of $75,000. The town dedicated the new bridge on October 26, 1935, with a large event.

The Depot Street Bridge, also known as Connecticut Bridge No. 3788, received extensive repairs and was repainted its original silver-gray color in 1986. The bridge was painted its current green color in the early 2000s. (Note that the bridge was never painted red, as depicted in several town seal images.)

The Depot Street Bridge is listed in the National Register of Historic Places, having received this designation on March 7, 2007.

MATTHIES PARK

JEWEL OF THE NAUGATUCK VALLEY

While other towns in the Naugatuck Valley may disagree on certain things, most agree that "the jewel" is Matthies Park. Nowhere else is there such a beautiful and pristine area of woodlands, pond and nature trails. Originally 326 acres of mostly untouched woodlands, the Matthies property was one of several "vacation cottages" Bernard Matthies owned in and around Connecticut.

As noted in the biography of Bernard Matthies commissioned by the Beacon Falls Park & Recreation Commission, Matthies would over a period of thirty-six years purchase all of the nearly 326 acres of land that made up his vacation retreat. The last 55-acre section was purchased in 1959 from the Carrington and Gomberwicz families. This eastern border of the entire parcel included the property where Woodland Regional High School was eventually built.

Located in Beacon Falls on the Oxford border, the property was purchased by the Town of Beacon Falls in 1972 as the potential site for a high school for the students of Regional School District No. 16 (Beacon Falls, Prospect, Connecticut). The original 326-acre parcel was purchased by the town for the sum of $150,000. The property, a portion of which is in the town of Oxford, consists of a pond (Carrington Pond) with a house on a man-made island, several miles of stone sluiceways that feed spring waters into the pond, a boathouse and a dam that was completed around 1936. It took about fifteen years to complete the construction.

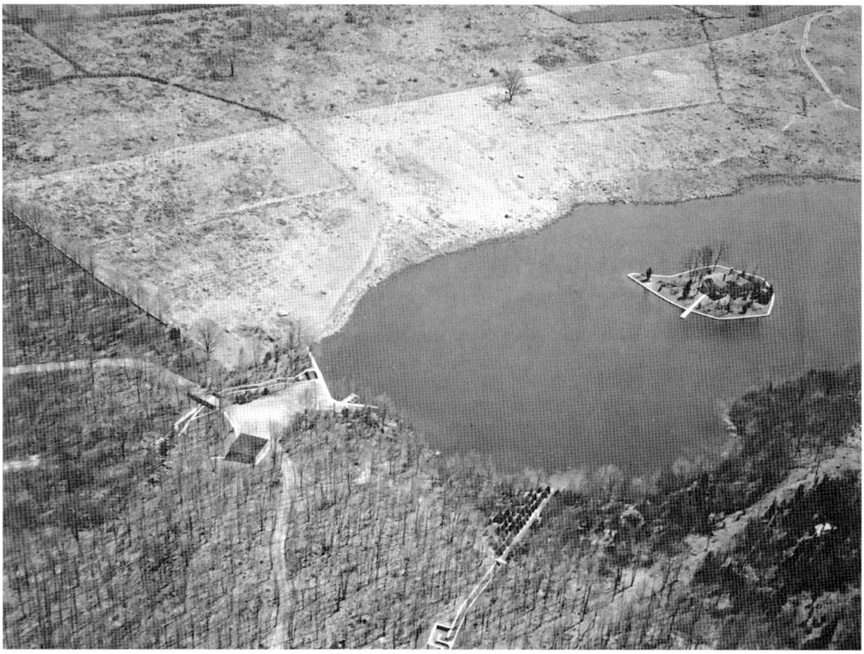

Circa 1940 aerial photo of Carrington Pond at the Matthies summer retreat. *Courtesy of the Beacon Falls Historical Society.*

Mr. Matthies was born on January 27, 1892, and was a lifelong resident of Seymour, Connecticut. The Matthies family have rich and deep roots into the area's colonial past. The Matthies family are related to the Woosters, who were early founders of Derby, Connecticut, and the Putnams of Salem, Massachusetts, from the 1630s.

Mr. Matthies was part of a notable family line of industrialists in the lower Naugatuck Valley. The Seymour Manufacturing Company was founded circa 1878 by his grandfather William Henry Harrison Wooster. Bernard Matthies followed in his grandfather's and father's footsteps, holding several positions after he returned from service during World War I.

Beyond the Seymour Manufacturing Company, Bernard Matthies filled positions at the American Copper Corporation and was a key member of the Colonial Air Lines (Bethany, Connecticut), which was one of the first airmail transport services in the country. He was the proprietor of Rimmon View Farm and later a vice-president of the Phosphor Bronze Corporation, a subsidiary of Seymour Manufacturing.

Bernard Matthies's career spanned more than fifty-five years, working across multiple Connecticut metal manufactures, in banking and finance, in petroleum refining industries and at a local utility, the Seymour Water Company.

Beginning in the mid-1920s, Mr. Matthies began acquiring the parcels that eventually made up his 326-acre vacation retreat. Bordered by Rimmon Hill Road on the east, Pinesbridge Road (State Route 42) on the north, Chestnut Tree Hill Road on the west and the "old abandoned road" to the south, the property included Hemp Swamp and Hemp Swamp Brook. Matthies built a seven-acre pond fed by a complex system of canals and sluiceways. In the middle of the new pond, a small half-acre island was constructed along with a one-and-a-half-story wood-frame house. The house is unused today, and the town is seeking funds to rehab the structure, along with the remainder of the parklands.

In 1999, the Towns of Beacon Falls and Prospect finally approved constructing a new eight-hundred-student high school on fifty-five acres along the eastern edge of the Matthies Park Property. The school opened in the fall of 2001.

Another notable feature/structure on the property is a brick pump house. This roughly fifteen-by-twenty-foot structure features a turbine-driven pump, which Matthies used to supplement water to feed the pond during dry summers. It was estimated that this pump and well might push more than one thousand gallons a minute into the adjacent sluice when in operation.

The paved road that meanders northward from Carrington Pond leads to several "settling ponds," which filter leaves and sediment from the water. This is Hemp Swamp Brook, from which some water is diverted to the pond, and the primary stream flows eventually into the Naugatuck River at Pinesbridge. This engineered system—consisting of the settling ponds, canals, sluiceways and natural springs feeding Carrington Pond—is a marvel to watch as water, following the natural topography of the land, gently flows down the nearly three-fourths of a mile into the pond.

Bernard Matthies was a taskmaster and demanded quality work. Apparently, on several occasions, he demanded that the work being performed be ripped out and redone. The Bernard Matthies biography cuts straight to the point: "The result is a unique and historically significant example of landscape development and engineering, the likes of which rarely are found on a private estate."

THE FLOOD OF 1955

No history of Beacon Falls would be complete without mentioning the most remembered disaster that hit the Naugatuck Valley area of Connecticut and Beacon Falls. The "Black Friday Flood" has been documented in numerous books, news articles and documentary videos.

Hurricane Connie: August 11, 1955

Connie hit the eastern coastline of the United States as a major storm, with Category 1 wind gusting upward of 100 miles per hour. During its path to the mainland, Connie reached as high as Category 4 strength, with recorded winds around 140 miles per hour. It wandered around the northwestern Atlantic for a number of days before hitting land in North Carolina. While the storm weakened to below hurricane strength as it moved inland on August 13, it merged with another low-level trough and turned toward the Northeast, dumping inches of water.

Wind was not the challenge when the hurricane reached Connecticut—it was the rain. Three to five inches of rain descended on New York City and Connecticut. The main thrust of the storm stayed to the west of Connecticut, but the combination of wind, rain and the previous months' drought conditions meant that water did not just run off—it saturated the ground.

Hurricane Diane and Black Friday: August 18 and August 19, 1955

Diane was the real challenge to the already rain-soaked ground and swollen rivers. Much like its sister Connie, which struck land just five days earlier, Diane hit land in North Carolina as a Category 1 hurricane on August 17, with sustained winds under 105 miles per hour.

The mid-Atlantic states, North Carolina and Virginia, did not suffer the brunt of Hurricane Diane. Although downgraded to a tropical storm, it was Connecticut that suffered much more than from the precipitation from Connie. Diane dropped a record sixteen-plus inches of rain over a two-day period as it reentered the Atlantic (and its warm summer waters) below New York City. The additional moisture unleashed torrents of rain that swelled rivers and lakes, which in turn caused many dams to collapse, causing the floods that devastated the Naugatuck Valley.

Across the New England states, 206 dams were damaged or destroyed by the rainfall. Nationwide, nearly 7,000 people were injured; Diane killed at least 184 people. The exact number killed in the Naugatuck Valley is still not determined, but it is estimated as 20 to 30 in Naugatuck and Waterbury, with at the time hundreds missing.

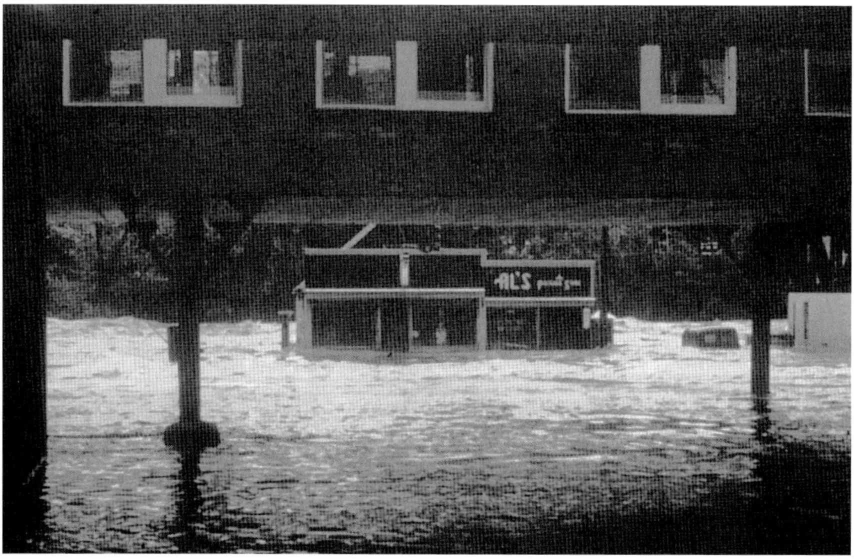

Floodwaters rise on Main Street during the Flood of '55. The H.W. Wilcox Patent Medicines was one of the buildings that survived the flood. *Photo by Harold W. Wilcox, author's collection.*

Beacon Falls suffered greatly. As reported in the *Waterbury Republican* newspaper, Pinesbridge Cemetery was destroyed, with gravestones and caskets shuffled over the cemetery grounds. Mr. John McGeever, a volunteer firefighter and at the time a caretaker of the cemetery, stated, "We did not have an accurate map of the cemetery and all we could do was line the caskets in a row. Maybe it says Smith on the stone, but maybe it's a Curtis in the casket."

Many of the homes in Pinesbridge were heavily damaged. Water overran the banks on Main Street, and houses and businesses were inundated with four and a half feet of water. My grandfather Harold Wilcox, who owned the Wilcox drugstore in the center of town, stated that the water "reached the top of the lunch counter" during the height of the flood.

LEGENDS, MYTHS AND STORIES ASSOCIATED WITH BEACON FALLS

Beacon Falls in the Movies

Beacon Falls, like every town across the state and country, has its stories and legends surrounding events that occurred there—or maybe they did not actually happen but nonetheless are fun in the telling.

Beacon Falls had its fifteen minutes of fame in the movies. The first of two movies that come to mind is *Jackknife*, staring Robert De Niro, Ed Jones and Kathy Baker, which was filmed in 1989. About fifteen minutes into the film, there is a scene where the car they are driving in as they are heading to a place to go fishing is viewed on Route 8 heading north toward Naugatuck. Slightly blurred in the background along the side of the southbound lane is a road sign for "Beacon Falls." For those who drive this road, the High Rock State Park is another familiar sight seen in the movie. Another scene was filmed on North Main Street at what was at the time a package store; most recently, it was a real estate office. This scene may have been left on the cutting room floor, as I do not remember it in the film.

Another movie that many will remember was *Revolutionary Road*, starring Leonard DiCaprio and Kate Winslet and filmed in 2007. In a scene early into the movie, DiCaprio's and Winslet's characters are driving at night and pull off the road at a roadside stand along what the movie calls "Route 12." It was actually Route 8, opposite the Gelmini Farm, also known recently as "Joe's Farm" on Lopus Road. As the municipal historian, I was called in to find a number of objects to be used in the background. During filming, many local residents attempted to view the filming, and on several occasions, people were asked to remove themselves from the Lopus Road Bridge over Route 8, as the producer of the movie was not sure if they might be seen in the distance. The roadside stand, which was built on site, was given to Joe's Farm and was used as its farm stand for a number of years.

THE LEGENDS AND STORIES OF HIGH ROCK

The following tales and legends have parallel themes and cast of characters tied to High Rock. There is an area within the current park that is called "Squaw Rock," and the legends tell the story of how it was named. First up are three different versions of the same story, which perhaps shows that even in the 1700s and 1800s, people played "telephone" with what they heard when repeating their version of the legend. The fourth and last story is named "Che-Wa-Wale." All four follow the same premise that there was a chieftain, Toby, with a daughter (some called her a princess); she found herself in danger, and three of the stories feature a disastrous outcome, but one has a "fairy tale" ending. All take place in or around the High Rock and Pinesbridge areas of Beacon Falls.

The first story is a version of the "serpent story," as told on many a night to anyone who would listen by the town's first municipal historian, Michael "Mike" Krenesky (1920–2003).

The High Rock Serpent

Every year, there are two days to be (or maybe not to be) at High Rock State Park in the Naugatuck State Forest. On those two days, March 20 and November 20, at midnight, a seven-headed serpent crawls out of a crevice in the face of the rock and gazes longingly up and down the Naugatuck Valley. It is said that on the forehead of the large center head of this creature reposes a brilliant jewel of immeasurable value—if anyone were courageous and agile enough to attempt to remove it. (AUTHOR'S NOTE: As with all legends, small portions of the tale tend to differ. In this version, the latter date of November 20 is suspect, as you will read in another version of this story soon enough.)

Now of course, there are skeptical people who will dismiss the whole thing as fable, a figment of imagination or an outright lie. But those people are to be pitied. They are the blind, disillusioned cynics who deny the existence of Santa Claus or Irish leprechauns despite the mountain of eyewitness evidence supporting both.

About three hundred years ago, a party of white traders, perhaps from the Massachusetts Bay Colony, sailed up the Naugatuck River to barter their trinkets for beaver pelts that the local Native Americans had gathered. It is told that the sachem of the Indians, Chief Toby, had a beautiful daughter and that one of the traders had a keen eye for beauty. He offered Chief Toby a quart of rum if the chief would allow his daughter to depart with him for Boston.

That sounded like a fair exchange to the chief, as rum was hard to come by and there was no shortage of daughters, so he agreed to the swap. But the willful daughter would not agree to the trade unless she could have a pint of rum for herself. Being a kindly man, her father agreed, while at the same time lamenting the avarice of his offspring.

The Indian maiden made short work of the rum. It made her light-headed as well as light-footed—off she ran into the forest, with the trader and Chief Toby hot on her heels. Eventually, she reached the lip of the ledge at the top of High Rock, also known as Squaw Rock. Before her pursuers could reach her, she fell to her death.

Chief Toby, peering over the precipice at the lifeless body of his beautiful daughter, was overwhelmed with remorse. His rum jug was still in his hand, and he was about to throw it over the cliff when he thought better of it and drained it first. Then he pitched it after his daughter in grief and anger. Where it fell and shattered, a huge boulder thrust out of the earth—a monument to the unfortunate girl and a warning against the evils of rum.

Indian legend tells that the spirit of a dead Indian returns in animal form—because of that, an Indian hunter always apologizes to any animal he must kill for food, in the event that he is slaying a reincarnated member of his tribe.

The rum-loving daughter of Chief Toby returns as the serpent with seven heads, with the center head adorned with a precious stone. The stone being valuable, the prophecy promises great wealth to anyone who can wrest the jewel from the serpent and carry it as a talisman of good luck. If you are interested in collecting this jewel, remember that there are only two days in a year that the opportunity presents itself. Remember the dates and good luck!

The Legends and Stories of High Rock (Version 2)

The following alternate versions come from Samuel Orcutt's 1882 book *Indians of the Housatonic and Naugatuck Valleys*. In these versions of the story, there is no serpent, but they serve as warnings nonetheless.

> *Some two hundred years ago, when Indian maidens wandered over the mountains, or paddled their light canoes, and sang like Laughing Water, while thinking of a hunter from another tribe and country. Traders (probably Dutch from New Amsterdam) came from the coast, and sought to bribe the Chieftain Toby, with a quart of rum, to give his daughter to the traders. But she, being as the sequel proves romantically inclined, begged that she might have one-half of the rum before giving her consent. She drank it and fled from her father's wigwam. Failing to return soon, Toby and his warriors started in pursuit of her. Coming out upon the top of Toby's Rock, and looking across the Glen, Toby discovered his daughter standing alone upon Squaw Rock. The maiden perceiving that she was discovered sprang to the edge of the cliff, precipitated herself to the base of the rock, and was killed. After witnessing the death of his daughter, Toby dispatched his warriors to the village, to take from the traders the jug of rum. It was taken to the top of the Rock and thrown thence into the center of the river; when, behold from the spot where it struck, there sprang instantly a huge boulder, which remains to this day—a warning to all future Tobies, who may be disposed to sell their daughters for rum.*

The Legends and Stories of High Rock (Version 3)

This last of three versions of the High Rock legend, as reported by Orcutt, gets to the same conclusion, but with a different twist.

> *Long years ago, when the country belonged to the Indians, a certain chief became enamored of a dusky maiden of another tribe and sought to make her his squaw, but she was not in favor of this plan, and one evening, when the chief came a wooing, she took to her heels and made straight for the summit of this cliff. She was closely pursued, and on reaching the edge of the precipice found herself almost within the grasp of the deserted lover. Escape in the direction whence she came was cut off; beneath her yawned the dreadful abyss. Breathing a prayer to the Great Spirit, she threw herself*

from the brink, and the next moment was a shapeless mass upon the rocks below. Hence came the name "Squaw Rock."

Orcutt goes on to report:

The Spirit of the maiden does not rest well, whatever was the cause of her death, her spirit appears on September and March 20th at midnight in the form of a snake with four or seven heads with a large "carbuncle" on each head. It is said should one capture on of the carbuncles, it will make him or her fabulously rich.

To these versions of the story, the following is one additional ending that you the reader can accept or dispute—it goes a long way toward understanding how Beacon Falls was named.

Many of the group that attempted to stop the Indian maiden when she darted from the chief's wigwam, waited at the bottom of the cliff and watched in horror as the events transpired. When the maiden fell or jumped as the stories vary, we hear for the first time a possible name of the maiden— Beacon. *As she fell to the ground below the cliff, one of the observers was heard to shout, "Beacon falls."*

The Tale of "Che-Wa-Wale"

The story of Che-Wa-Wale was originally published in the *Philadelphia Native American*, author and publication date unknown. The story was reprinted in the third volume of the *Portland Transcript* of Portland, Maine (Saturday March 1, 1845), and is attributed to David M. Stone. The *Portland Transcript* was a literary newspaper of the mid-nineteenth century, described as "devoted to literature, arts and sciences, morals, news of the day, etc." The paper printed every Saturday and was published by William H. Jerries. The story is reproduced here in its entirety as it appeared on March 1, 1845, including the grammar, punctuation and spelling that was used in the mid-nineteenth century:

No person who has followed the course of the Naugatuc, as it dashes down among the hills in the western part of New Haven County Conn, can have failed to remark the range of the bold, bluff mountains that wall in on the west, just above Pine's Bridge, in Oxford.

Rising abruptly from the water, which is frequently the deepest at their very base, they tower aloft in many places to the height of 200 feet, showing a ragged front of massive rocks, that look as though they were piled up by the hand of Nature, when she would try her skill at a huge rampart.

In fact, many of those peaks are, near their summits, composed entirely of large rocks, heaped together, with scarcely a particle of earth, thus affording numberless caverns and subterranean passages, where, before the settlement of the neighboring country, the wild beast disputed possession with the lawless and abandoned who fled thither or protection from the strong arm of the law.

In the days when our paper issues, *"Continental money," as they were called, were the principal currency of the country, these rocks were the abode of a gang of counterfeiters, who divided with the proper authorities the labor of preparing the representative of value received.—There was also living near one of the highest peaks (Called Devil's Leap) an Indian of the Newanset tribe, who, when his tribe were scattered, partly by a wasting disease and partly by a cruel war waged against them, built him a hut in this lonely place, that he might still dwell near the graves of his fathers. He went by the name of Toby, and the rocks are called Toby's Rocks to this day.*

As the "Continental" issued by this gang gave no small trouble to the colony which had branched our from the Quinnipiac settlement, they made many ineffectual efforts to stop it; owing, however, to the wilderness of the country, and to the secure retreat the caves afforded to the refugees, the law had no power over them.—Emissaries they had, doubtless, to distribute their fraudulent notes, but this was done so adroitly that they could not be detected. They hunted very little themselves, and it was Toby's chief employment to supply them with game. He cared little whether their trade was lawful or not, so long as they paid him sterling coin.

Toby's wife, like the rest of her tribe during the great sickness, had passed away, and yet he was not alone. Che-Wa-Wale, "the bright light," kept the darkness of sorrow from her father's wigwam.—Beautiful was she, as the fairest of the red men's daughters; and such a fund of kindness and good humor was there in her heart—such music in her laugh—such a fairy lightness in her step, and above all, such a bewitching brightness in her coal black eye, that many a hunter turned from his path to eat venison in the sun-light of her presence.

But Che-Wa-Wale had a heart only for her father, her brightest smiles were for his cheer, her lightest step about his bed of repose. Even the leader of the gang among the rocks had wooed her for his wild home, but she refused to hear him—and when he urged her to more than was seemly, she only meekly replied: "My father dwells alone, where his fathers were many; if Che-Wa-

Wale goes, there is not one left to cook his meat or spread his mat as he comes from the chase. I cannot go. Why should his dwelling be dark?"

But Jack Harling was not a man to be said nay, *and there was an evil eye watching her from that hour!*

About a month after this occurrence, a party of twenty men, headed by Isaac Churchill, left the settlement near the junction of the Naugatuc and Housatonic rivers, on purpose to arrest the gang at the rocks. Their march being noised about, and undertaken in open day, the counterfeiters had notice of it, and when the party invaded the place, they were safely concealed in a large cave formed among the rocks.

The writer visited this cave in the Spring of 1839, and although it was much filled up by falling in of the loose stones that were torn off from the surrounding rocks, yet its entrance and course were easy to perceive. There were originally many entrances to the large room in the cave, but as one exception they were so small as to admit one person at a time, and that on hands and knees; and as they were long dark passages, full of turnings and crossings, they were seldom used except on occasions of great emergency, and in fact could not be traced to the cave itself, except by chance, or by someone well acquainted with its windings.

The principal entrance was open to the warmest rays of the noonday sun, and yet few would have found it. Near to the top of the mountain, so near as not to be commanded bay any part of it, rose a large rock about fourteen feet high, so abrupt and smooth at that time as not to be scaled except by a ladder, and yet not above twelve feet in diameter at the base. On the top of this rock was an opening, resembling a sunken well, about seventeen feet deep, which led off by a short passage from the bottom of the principal vault. In this a ladder was kept, and when any one was expected in, someone was on the watch for his signal, and going up the ladder, drew it up after him, and let it down the outside to his companion.

At my visit in '39, I found the entrance overshadowed by a small sapling that had struggled up between the rocks outside, and having after prodigious labor and many falls, clambered up the rock, I seized a branch and thoughtlessly swung myself down the opening. I found my farther progress checked by the filling up of the principal cavity; the branch that let me down safely, had sprung back, and I was in prison! I succeeded after two hours hard labor, in digging myself out, but had no desire to explore farther; my curiosity was quite cooled!

To return from this digression: After diligent search of the neighborhood, the party under Churchill came to the conclusion that the counterfeiters were concealed in the rocks; but which of the many openings in the rock led to their place of concealment, or how to approach them, they could not tell.

Toby was brought from his hut, and alternately offered threats and bribes to betray them, but the Indian was immovable.

The party, although accustomed to all perils of a hunter's life, shrank from the danger of losing themselves underground:

Impatient of this delay, Churchill divested himself of his outer garments, and without taking the precaution, like Putnam, to fasten a cord to his leg, entered what seemed one of the principal openings. No one had the courage to follow and he never returned! *As his body never was found, it is supposed either that he squeezed himself into an aperture too small to admit of his returning, or else that he lost his way among the windings and perished by famine. The party, without accomplishing their purpose, returned dispirited to their homes.*

Encouraged by the safety of their retreat, the gang again commenced working their press, but Harding seemed less attentive to the business than was his wont. Ever since Che-wa-wale had refused his suit, he had mediated other means to secure her as his own. He would not have hesitated to take her by main force, but he feared to trust the whole band with such an enterprise, for hardened as they were in their wickedness, all who had visited Toby's wigwam had done homage to the charms of "the bright light." Neither did he wish to offend Toby, for he was a useful ally, whose favor it was important to retain. His plan was one or two select companions, to carry Che-wa-wale to an apartment in the cave, during the absence of her father, and then by shrewdly disposing Indian signs about the hut, to put Toby on the wrong scent, persuading him, either that she had eloped with some favored lover, or been carried off by force, to light another wigwam; for the fame of her beauty had spread among even distant tribes.

Toby was away, hunting the deer, and Che-wa-wale was alone, working a belt that was one day to become precious in his eyes, as his daughter's gift. She was sitting near the open door, singing snatches of old war songs, she had heard when a child—for the council fires of her tribe had long ceased to be kindled—when a shadow fell across the threshold, and as she looked up, Harding entered the wigwam. She had lived in her innocence so entirely unmolested, that she never had feared, even the sight of a strange wildness in his eye that startled her.

Rising as he entered, she said, "My father has drawn his bow for the deer, and Che-wa-wale is alone; why has my white brother come?"

"A bundle of bright shawls and gay ribbons have come from the settlement, if you will come up to the rock and see them, the brightest shall be yours!"

"Che-wa-wale," replied the maiden, "has no eye for her white brother's gift; when her father brings home the deer, he will buy what she needs."

"By heavens you shall go with me, girl, as proud as you are!" said Harding, bursting forth in rage, and ere she could stir, he seized her in his arms, and after a moment's struggle, bore her from the hut.—Calling to his two men whom he had concealed near, he tied her hands, and bound the belt she was working around her mouth and they carried her to cave. Returning immediately with a piece of her dress he had torn off, and an old moccasin he found in the cave, he went some distance in an opposite direction from the hut, and hanging the shred of cloth on a bush, he dropped the moccasin near it, to lead pursuit in that direction.

Scarcely bowed by the weight of the deer he had killed, Toby strode to the door of the wigwam, but Che-wa-wale was not there to welcome him. Throwing down the carcass, he sprang in and searched the hut, but it was empty. Looking carefully around the entrance, he could easily see signs there of struggling feet, but the rocky path beyond was too hard to give a trail that could be followed. He sat down on the threshold, where she had welcomed his return for so many years and covered his face in the agony of despair.

Just at this moment, William Conrad, a young hunter of great daring and trained to the woods from his youth, came up to the hut, and laying his hand on the Indian's shoulder, cried out, "What ails thee, Toby? Where is thy daughter, Che-wa-wale, that she has no greeting for the weary?"

Raising his head slowly, and gazing listlessly into the hunter's face, as if he were in a dream, Toby replied, "The light has gone out in the old man's dwelling! Che-wa-wale met me not as I came from the chase; my daughter has been stolen from me, and I can find no trail!"

"And thou are setting here idle when this outrage has been done! Has thy tomahawk no edge?" said young Conrad vehemently.

The suddenness as well as the severity of the blow, had for a moment stunned him, but now fully aroused, he assisted the young man in his search. It was not long before they found the piece of her dress, and the moccasin which Harding had dropped. As soon as he saw the make of the latter, Toby cried out—"It is as I thought; the dogs from the Ousatonic have come like a thief, and darkened my wigwam!"

"If they came with this," said Conrad, examining it attentively, "they must have brought it in their hands, for the dust is thick on the inside, and see, the thongs have been laced since it was worn! Now believe me, no red man was ever so stupid as to try such a trick as this; and I'll wager my head, that your white friends up at the rock are the villains after all!"

Leaving the young man at the hut, the old Indian started for the rocks. He found nothing on the way to confirm his suspicions, until he reached the tall rock, whence was the descent to the cave. Around the base of this were strewn the large beads that Che-wa-wale had worn around her neck from childhood. She had broken the string in her struggle, as they drew her up the ladder, and the beads had fallen unnoticed. But they did not escape the eagle-eye of the father.—He had kissed them often as she had lain on his breast, and he knew them every one!

Gathering them up in silence he returned to his wigwam. Both Toby and his friend saw the uselessness of attempting anything further without help, and fatigued as they both were, they yet immediately started for the settlement. It was some time after dark then they arrived, but they quietly sat at work to collect a force, and before midnight they were on their march back to the rocks with more than thirty well-armed men.

They reached the entrance to the cave before break of day; and guided by the Indian, they planted their ladders in silence against the rocks. They were well furnished with torches, and had there been no accident, would have surprised the whole gang, but in the hurry of descent, too many pressed upon the first ladder, which gave way with an echoing crash.—The noise alarmed the outlaws, who rushing through the various outlets of the cave most of them escaped.

Che-wa-wale, after she had been forced into the cave pleaded earnestly to be spared, if but one day, from the disgrace which awaited her; and Harding consented, in the hope that he might then win her without violence. The little vault he occupied contained but one bed which he gave up to her, stretching himself at its foot.

She had not slept, and the first alarm, hoping it might be for her rescue, sprang for the entrance, but Harding was watching, and taking her in his strong arms, forced her back.

As the party approached, each with his torch, following one another as closely as possible, Toby, who was in advance, caught a glimpse of his daughter struggling with the villain. Harding, who saw the Indian, and now comprehended the nature of the attack, in the madness of disappointed passion, drew his knife, determined that she should at least die with him. Toby had no weapon but his tomahawk—he was not near enough to use it, and there was not room to throw it. With one wild shriek for help, Che-wa-wale fell back upon her bed—the knife was pointed at her breast—when the report of a pistol rang through the vault. Conrad, who followed the Indian, had seen the danger—and averted it! The counterfeiter lay dead at her feet! Much booty was found in the cave and the breaking up of the gang is now a matter of history.

There was light again in the Indian's wigwam, for Che-wa-wale sang there once more her old familiar songs and poured out there on the bosom of her deliverer the gratitude of her pure and thankful heart. But when this was over, why did Conrad still linger around the hut; and why came he so often with his gifts for "the bright light"?

Gentle reader, can you guess?

THE FERRYBOAT

The Naugatuck River was a wild river before the 1960s, when numerous flood control measures started to be developed to control its wrath. There was significant flooding on the Naugatuck River in 1927, 1936 and 1949. While the 1955 flood is what everyone remembers for its extensive damage, the 1949 flooding was nearly as destructive in Beacon Falls, specifically for the area of Pinesbridge.

The following are passages of a story printed in a local newspaper, assumed to be the *Evening Sentinel*, on February 25 and again in 1949 (another presumption, information is unknown). Mr. Richard Houseknecht (born in 1868 in Pennsylvania) was fifty-eight years old, sixty-seven and eighty during the aforementioned flood dates. He resided on Old Pinesbridge Road below what was then the two bridges and roadway that traversed the river.

The images here were taken by Mr. Art Marasco, a well-known area photographer, on January 3, 1949, when the Naugatuck River again reached flood stage.

Setting the scene for this story, prior to building the current bridge that crosses the Naugatuck River, the path to cross the river was much different than one might expect. A narrow road with two small bridges and a spit of land between them made up the road that traversed the river. This roadway passed under the Naugatuck Railroad tracks, using the railroad bridge or underpass that is found at the current entrance to Toby's Park. It tracked onto Lopus Road in an area called the "Rabbit Hole"—the location of the oldest house in Beacon Falls, the Riggs House. It is the third house from the entrance to the park.

If one were to enter what is today Toby's Park and walk or drive straight ahead about twenty yards to the river instead of immediately turning right toward the pond, you would find the only other remaining infrastructure that was part of the original road and bridge.

The story is about man's desire and efforts to battle Mother Nature at her worse, with man's ingenuity and determination to control these forces of nature. Titled "Ferryboat Is to Be Placed on Naugatuck River Where Bridge Was Washed Away," the article tells the tale of Mr. Houseknecht's attempt to reestablish the route across the river:

> *Primarily Mr. Houseknecht's object in building a boat was for the purpose of conveying wood from his property on the opposite side of the river, or the west bank, which is directly across from his home, to the east bank, which*

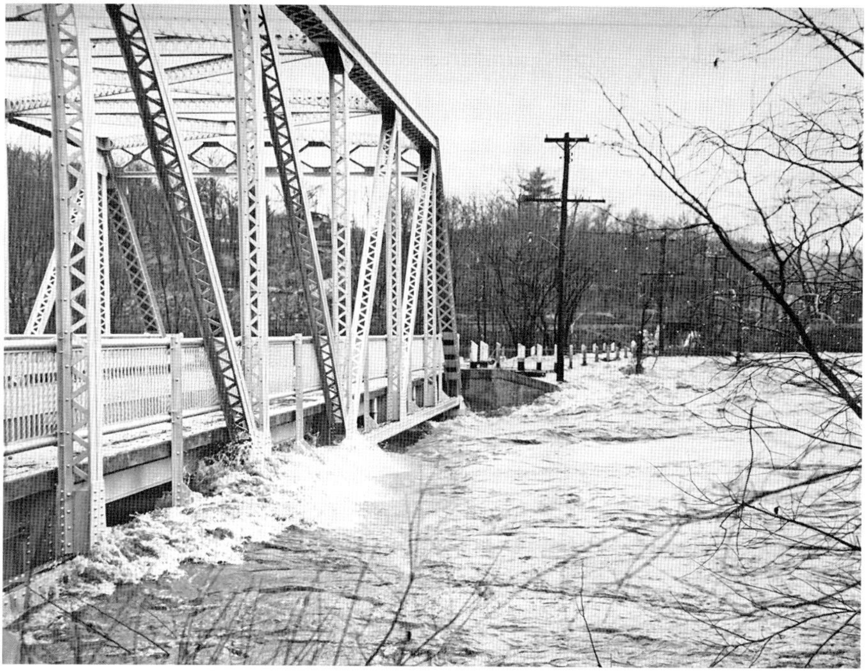

River water from the January 1949 flood crashes against the metal section of the roadway in the Pinesbridge area of Beacon Falls. *Courtesy of A. Marasco Photography, photo by Art Marasco.*

> *present conditions require a journey of about four miles, necessitating going to Beacon Falls and crossing of the river on the Center bridge and a rough travel over the West river on Lopez road, to get to a point 80 yards opposite from the starting point.*

It should be noted that, over time and depending on the source, the currently named Depot Street Bridge was also called "Center Bridge" or the "Bridge Street Bridge"—the former because it was considered the center of town and the latter for more self-explanatory reasons.

No pictures have surfaced of the boat that was being built, but the story describes it as "of the flat-bottomed scow type, and is about 20 feet long, and about four feet wide of very sturdy construction." Intended to be used to carry wood as described, it apparently included "seats" should any passengers want to cross the river.

The design for the boat meant allowed travel straight across or perpendicular to the course of the river on a cable hookup with a pulley attachment as a means of power.

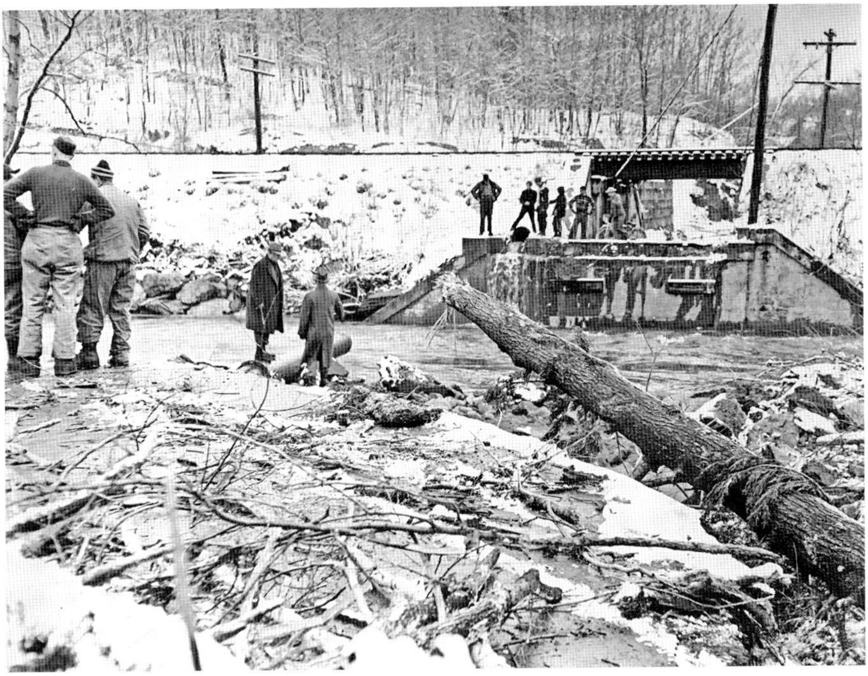

Residents view damage to the road and bridge in the aftermath of the January 1949 flood. *Courtesy of A. Marasco Photography, photo by Art Marasco.*

In Houseknecht one finds a very pleasing and hospitable character; a visit to his home reveals a house of excellent design and proportions built by himself, literally packed with antiques of all descriptions and numerous pieces and articles illustrative of his own ingenuity and efficient handiwork: chairs, tables, clocks, beds and various pieces of the woodworking type. Several of the articles in his possession range from 150 to 250 years of age.

With the destruction of the bridges across the river, and the inconvenience it presented to the residents and those who needed to travel between east and west, the State Highway Commission in the days and weeks following the flood began planning to replace the damaged sections with a permanent structure. Such repairs would begin later in the fall at the earliest, leaving those who wanted to travel the route of having "the preference of doing so either by boat or long way around through the center of town or through Seymour."

Credit was given to Mr. Houseknecht, "the long-entertained problem has been solved to some extent through the foresightedness and efforts of Mr.

Houseknecht. The scow will be ready for its 'maiden voyage' in about five days and will no doubt be a success."

There is no known reference in town records, nor future newspaper accounts, of the fate of the ferryboat.

Appendix I

SPECIAL ACT: INCORPORATION OF BEACON FALLS CONNECTICUT

Upon the petition of John Wolfe and others praying for the incorporation of a new town to be erected out of portions of the Towns of Bethany, Naugatuck, Seymour and Oxford as per petition on file which has been duly served and returned:—

Resolved by this Assembly:

Section 1. That all those parts of the Towns of Bethany, Naugatuck, Seymour and Oxford lying within the following described limits and boundaries, viz: beginning at a point on an old highway known as Blackberry Hill Road, in the Town of Bethany, which is intersected by a straight line extended and running on and in the northern boundary line of the homestead farm of Norman Peck, in Seymour, which boundary line is marked by a stone wall in part: thence running northerly in said old highway to a point about forty rods east of a dwelling house known as the Edward Buckingham house, thence north fourteen degrees east one hundred and eighty one and one half rods to a heap of stones on Perfins land (so called); thence north three and one half degrees east four hundred and twenty rods; thence north twenty nine degrees west to a point on Beacon Hill Brook, opposite the saw mill of Amos Hotchkiss, to a heap of stones: thence following said brook westerly to the Naugatuck River; thence following the Naugatuck River southerly to the mouth of Spruce Brook on the west bank of the same; thence following the town line northwesterly to a heap of stones which marks the boundary line between Oxford and Naugatuck; thence running southerly to a large oak stump known as Oak Tree Corner about eighty rods north of the dwelling of Stiles Fairfield; thence in a straight line southwest to Hemp Swamp Bridge so called; thence in a straight line to a heap of stones on the east side of Diamond Rock (so called), which marks the boundary between Seymour and Oxford, said last line being the district lines of Rimmon district; thence easterly and northerly following the Oxford and Seymour Town line to a point on Rock Rimmon in a line with said home farm of the said Norman Peck; thence following on said line which runs a little south of east in a straight line to the point of the beginning; with all inhabitants residing within said limits, be and in the same is hereby incorporated and erected into a new and separate Town by the name of Beacon Falls with the rights, honors, privileges and immunities and subject to all the duties and liabilities of other Towns in the State, with the right of sending one representative to the General Assembly of the State, and all those parts of the above mentioned Towns embraced in the foregoing limits to be and remain an independent Town with the name of Beacon Falls, by which name it shall hereafter be called and known.

Section 2. And said new Town shall pay its proportion according to the list of 1870 of all state, town, and other taxes now levied, and the collectors of said towns are hereby authorized to collect the same, of all debts existing against said Towns of Bethany, Naugatuck, Oxford and Seymour, and of all charges and expenses, and of all contracts for which said Towns are now or shall be hereafter be liable, by force of any contracts or claim now existing, except the expenses incurred by either of the aforesaid towns, in contesting this petition for said new Town.

Section 3. The poor of said Towns of Bethany, Naugatuck, Oxford and Seymour who were born within the limits hereby incorporated, and who have not by residence or otherwise gained an settlement elsewhere in this state than within said limits, shall be deemed inhabitants of said new town, and shall be maintained by the same, and said new Town shall be liable to maintain all such poor of the Towns of Bethany, Naugatuck, Oxford and Seymour as are and may be absent therefrom provided such persons at the time of their departure had a legal settlement in that part of Bethany, Naugatuck, Oxford and Seymour hereby incorporated in said new Town.

Section 4. All rights, property and estate of whatever name, nature, or description except the town house and records of said Towns, owned by, due, or belonging to the Towns of Bethany, Naugatuck, Oxford and Seymour or which hereafter accrue to said Towns by virtue of any claim, right or title now existing, shall belong to said new Town in proportion to the respective lists according to the grand lists of 1870.

Section 5. And the Town deposit fund of said Towns of Bethany, Naugatuck, Oxford and Seymour shall belong to, and be divided between said new Town as hereby incorporated and said Towns in proportion to the number of inhabitants of said Bethany, Naugatuck, Oxford and Seymour, and the inhabitance of the limits of that part taken from said Towns, and the number of paupers belonging to said new Town shall be ascertained and determined by and between the Selectmen of said new and the Selectmen of said Towns of Bethany, Naugatuck, Oxford and Seymour and if the Selectmen of said Towns of Bethany, Naugatuck, Oxford and Seymour cannot agree after the organization of said new Town, in the distribution of the paupers, funds, deposit funds, property and other matters to be settled between said Town, on, or before the first day of October 1871, then the Selectmen of said new Town of Beacon Falls and said Towns of Bethany, Naugatuck, Oxford and Seymour may apply to Lesnan W Cutler of Watertown, Sidney A. Downs of Derby and in the case they do not accept and serve, then in their stead Eli Curtis of Watertown and Thomas Ellams of Derby, who are hereby authorized and empowered to divide paupers, funds, deposit funds and property and settle all other matters to be settled between said Towns, growing out of this act of incorporation which division whether made by Selectmen or referees shall be final and conclusive on said Towns respectfully, and in the case said division shall be made by said referees, the selectmen of said Towns so disagreeing, shall first be duly notified of the time and place when and where said division shall be made, and all expenses of said services if rendered by said referees shall be paid by and between said new Town and said Towns of Bethany, Naugatuck, Oxford and Seymour (the Town or Towns disagreeing) according to the respective lists of said Towns, said lists, being the lists of A.D. 1870.

Section 6. Said new Town as hereby incorporated shall belong to and constitute a part of the 5th Senatorial district and shall also belong to and constitute a part of the probate district of Naugatuck.

Section 7. The first town meeting of said new Town shall be held in said Town of Beacon Falls on the first Monday of July 1871 at one o'clock in the afternoon, and Buell Buckingham or in his absence John Coe shall be moderator thereof, and said Buckingham and Coe or either of them shall warn said meeting, and all the inhabitances of the Town of Beacon Falls who are legal voters in the Town meeting, to meet at said time and place at some convenient room, by putting up a notice on the public sign post in said new Town, or upon each of the river bridges herein, and at such other places as they or either of them may deem proper, within the limits of said new Town at least 5 days before said meeting, and said new Town shall have all powers incidental to other Towns in this State a said first meeting, and full rights to act accordingly, and the Officers elected at such meeting shall hold their respective offices until others are appointed and qualified in their stead, and the justices of the peace, viz, those elected by said Town of Bethany, residing within the limits of said Town of Beacon Falls shall be deemed to be, and shall have the same power to act as fully as though they had been elected by said new Town of Beacon Falls.

Section 8. The fund now belonging to the Town of Oxford, for the support of Pines-bridge know as the "Clark Pines Bridge Fund" shall belong to said new Town within which said bridge is situated, and be kept and held by said new Town for the sole support of said bridge according to the object for which said fund was created, and said new Town shall indemnify and save Said Oxford harmless from costs, and litigation if any should arise in consequence of this act.

Approved, June 30, 1871.
State of Connecticut S.S.
Office of the Secretary of State

I hereby certify that the foregoing is a true copy of the record in this office. In testimony whereof, I have hereunto set my hand and affixed the Seal of said State at Hartford this the 30th day of June A.D. 1871.

Hiram Appelman
Secretary of State

Appendix II

BOARD OF SELECTMEN, 1871-PRESENT

Before 1940, the term of office for the Board of Selectmen was one year.

1871–1872	Stiles Clark James L. Wheeler Noyes Wheeler	1873	Buel Buckingham James A. Wheeler Herbert C. Baldwin
1874–1876	Buel Buckingham Herbert C. Baldwin Ransom Lounsbury	1877	Herbert C. Baldwin Charles B. Clark Andrew W. Culver
1878	Herbert C. Baldwin Ransom Lounsbury Noyes Wheeler	1879–1880	Herbert C. Baldwin Ransom Lounsbury David M. French
1881	Herbert C. Baldwin David M. French Noyes Wheeler	1882–1883	Herbert C. Baldwin Noyes Wheeler Andrew W. Culver
1884–1885	Herbert C. Baldwin Cornelius W. Munson Ransom Lounsbury	1886	Herbert C. Baldwin Cornelius Munson Daniel J. Carrington
1887	Herbert C. Baldwin Daniel J. Carrington Homer D. Bronson	1888	Herbert C. Baldwin Ransom Lounsbury Jerome Andrews

1889	Herbert C. Baldwin Emerson J. Terrell George T. Clark	1890	Herbert C. Baldwin George T. Clark Olin D. Buckingham
1891	Cornelius W. Munson Olin D. Buckingham George T. Clark	1892	Herbert C. Baldwin Cornelius W. Munson Olin D. Buckingham
1893	Cornelius W. Munson Olin D. Buckingham John L. Rice	1894	Cornelius W. Munson Olin D. Buckingham George T. Clark
1895	Cornelius W. Munson Olin D. Buckingham John L. Rice	1896	Cornelius W. Munson Daniel Carrington George T. Clark
1897	Cornelius W. Munson Carlos F. Kimpton George T. Clark	1898	Cornelius W. Munson John L. Rice George T. Clark
1899	John L. Rice George T. Clark Cornelius W. Munson	1900	Herbert C. Baldwin (resigned February 8, 1901) John L. Rice I Cornelius W. Munson
1901	William B. Hopwood Cornelius W. Munson Daniel J. Carrington	1902	William B. Hopwood Cornelius W. Munson Arthur Foetsch
1903	William B. Hopwood Cornelius W. Munson Olin D. Buckingham	1904	William B. Hopwood Cornelius W. Munson Olin D. Buckingham
1905	William B. Hopwood Cornelius W. Munson Olin D. Buckingham	1906	Cornelius Munson Milton Carrington Theodore Schmitz
1907	William Hopwood Cornelius Munson Jerome Andrews	1908	William Hopwood Cornelius Munson Theodore Schmitz
1909	William Hopwood Cornelius Munson Daniel J. Carrington	1910	Cornelius Munson Frank E. Bronson Theodore Schmitz

1911	Cornelius Munson Frank E. Bronson Daniel J. Carrington	1912	Cornelius Munson William Gallagher Daniel J. Carrington
1913	Cornelius Munson William Gallagher Daniel Carrington	1914	Cornelius Munson William Gallagher Daniel Carrington
1915	Cornelius Munson William Gallagher John Noe	1916	Cornelius Munson William Gallagher John Noe
1917	Cornelius Munson William Gallagher Theodore Schmitz	1918	Cornelius Munson William Gallagher Louis A. Zick
1919	B.E. Wakefield William Gallagher Theodore Schmitz	1920	B.E. Wakefield William Gallagher Theodore Schmitz
1921	B.E. Wakefield William Gallagher Ludwig Zick	1922	B.E. Wakefield William Gallagher Ludwig Zick
1923	B.E. Wakefield William Gallagher Ludwig Zick	1924	B.E. Wakefield William Gallagher Ludwig Zick
1925	B.E. Wakefield William Gallagher Theodore Schmitz	1926	William Gallagher Frank E. Bronson Theodore Schmitz
1927	William Gallagher Oscar J. Johnson Theodore Schmitz	1928	Theodore Schmitz Oscar Johnson William Hopwood
1929	Theodore Schmitz Oscar Johnson James Rourke	1930	Theodore Schmitz Oscar Johnson James Rourke
1931	Theodore Schmitz Oscar Johnson James Rourke	1932	Theodore Schmitz Oscar Johnson William Gallagher
1933	Theodore Schmitz Oscar Johnson James Rourke	1934	Theodore Schmitz Oscar Johnson Christian Heiss

1935	Christian Heiss Sherman Stocker Theodore Schmitz	1936	Christian Heiss Sherman Stocker Theodore Schmitz
1937	Christian Heiss Austin Ford Theodore Schmitz	1938	Theodore Schmitz Fred Schmitz Ralph E. Upright Austin Ford
1939	Austin Ford Ralph E. Upright Fred Schmitz	1940	Austin Ford Ralph E. Upright William Dubay
1941	Austin Ford Ralph E. Upright Joseph Trzaski	1942	Austin Ford Ralph E. Upright Clarence Carlson
1943	Ralph E. Upright Christian Heiss Conleth E. Kiernan	1944	Conleth E. Kiernan Christian Heiss Ralph E. Upright
1945	Ralph E. Upright Christian Heiss Conleth E. Kiernan	1946	Frank W. Semplenski Edward J. Smith Ralph E. Upright
1947	Frank W. Semplenski Edward J. Smith Harold J. Benz	1948	Frank Semplenski Edward J. Smith Harold J. Benz

In 1949, the term of office for the Board of Selectmen was changed to two years.

1949	Frank Semplenski Edward J. Smith Wilfred Swan	1951	Frank Semplenski Edward J. Smith George Leeper
1953	Frank Semplenski Edward J. Smith George Leeper	1955	Frank Semplenski Edward J. Smith Louis Esposito
1957	John Woelflein Patsy DelVecchio Edward Smith	1959	Pat DelVecchio John Woelflein Rodney Vardon

1961	Pat DelVecchio Edward Bea Kermit Molleur	1963	Pat DelVecchio Edward Bea James Greene
1965	Pat DelVecchio Edward Bea James Greene	1967	James Greene Edward Betkoski Francis Keith
1969	James Greene Louis Esposito Garry Fuoco	1971	James Greene Garry Fuoco Louis Esposito
1973	Garry Fuoco John Betkoski Leonard D'Amico	1975	Garry Fuoco John Betkoski Leonard D'Amico
1977	Leonard D'Amico George Howe John Betkoski	1979	Leonard D'Amico David Scott George Howe
1981	Leonard D'Amico James Greene John Betkoski III	1983	Leonard D'Amico James Greene John Betkoski III
1985	Leonard D'Amico James Greene John Betkoski III	1987	Leonard D'Amico James Greene Louis Poeta
1989	Leonard D'Amico James Greene Louis Poeta	1991	Leonard D'Amico Susan A. Cable Jack Levine
1993	Leonard D'Amico Susan A. Cable Leonard Greene	1995	Susan A. Cable David Scott Richard Rydzik
1997	Susan A. Cable David Scott Richard Rydzik	1999	Susan A. Cable David Scott Richard Rydzik
2001	Richard Milhalcik Richard Rydzik Susan A. Cable	2003	Susan A. Cable Donald Molleur Arthur Daigle
2005	Susan A. Cable Gerard F. Smith Dominick S. Sorrentino	2007	Susan A. Cable Michael A. Krenesky Dominick S. Sorrentino

2009	Susan A. Cable Dominick S. Sorrentino Michael A. Krenesky	2011	Gerald F. Smith David D'Amico Christopher Bielik
2013	Christopher Bielik Peter Betkoski Dominick Sorrento	2015	Christopher Bielik Peter Betkoski Michael A. Krenesky
2017	Christopher Bielik Michael A. Krenesky Peter Betkoski	2019	Gerard F. Smith Michael A. Krenesky Christopher Bielik

Appendix III

BEACON FALLS CHRONOLOGY

In 1999, my father, Michael Krenesky, self-published a chronological history of the town of Beacon Falls. In this work, he documented important dates and events that occurred over the period from 1639 to 1998. Having made updates, I include the revised text here as further reference related to the history of Beacon Falls.

1639: Early Roots

1639 Milford, Connecticut, is settled from the New Haven Bay Colony. The northern boundary, purchased from American Indians, is Beacon Hill Brook.

1665 Paugasett Indians sell land, piece by piece, to Derby settlers until town boundaries reached Waterbury. Beacon Hill Brook is the boundary between Waterbury and Derby, later Naugatuck and Beacon Falls.

1675 The twelve families at Paugasett are granted the privilege of a plantation that the court names Derby, which later becomes a separate town.

1676 Toby, an Indian boy, is secured by Major Ebenezer Johnson as a slave in New London.

1678 The earliest record of settlement in the Oxford district appears to be that of Ensign Samuel Riggs, who at a Derby Town Meeting held on January 14, 1678, is granted liberty to take up twenty acres of land at or near Rock Rimmon, in what is now Seymour on the west side of the Naugatuck River. Also that year, Major Ebenezer Johnson, Jeremiah Johnson and a few others purchased small tracts from American Indians at Rock Rimmon near Pinesbridge, the east side of the Naugatuck River. The Naugatuck River at one time was called the Paugasuck.

1680 Beacon Hill Brook marks Mattatuck's southern limit on the east side of the Naugatuck River. On the west side, a line runs over Twelve Mile Hill, where the stake marking is placed. Derby's northern boundary is twelve miles from Milford's northern boundary.

1686 Mattatuck changes its name to Waterbury.

1688 Toby, the Indian slave, is freed by Major Ebenezer Johnson.

1693 Through the influence of Major Ebenezer Johnson, Toby purchases for the consideration of ten pounds and a barrel of cider from the Paugasucks a large tract of mountain land in the northwestern part of town.

The 1700s

1700 Major Ebenezer Johnson and Ensign Riggs purchase more land from the Indians.

1703 Milford purchases more land from the Indians near Beacon Hill Brook.

1708 Johnson and Riggs divide their interests. Johnson takes land north of Pinesbridge Brook on the east side of the Naugatuck, and Riggs takes the west side of the Naugatuck River south of Pinesbridge Brook.

Ensign Riggs gives his son Ebenezer Riggs two hundred acres of choice land.

1709 A young native, Sarah, another maidservant of Colonel Johnson, desired as a wife by an Indian named Chetrenasut, purchases a tract of land called Nyumps for three pounds, ten shillings, bounded northerly by Beacon Hill Brook, easterly with Milford, westerly by Naugatuck River and southerly by Lebanon Brook.

1712 Ebenezer Riggs dies at little more than thirty years of age.

1713 The land sold to Toby is legally confirmed to him.

1721 Colonel Johnson divides land between his sons, Charles and Timothy.

1725 Timothy Johnson marries Abigail Brewster and settles on the Naugatuck River, below Pinesbridge Brook.

1730 Alexander Johnson, son of Timothy and Abigail, is born; he lives here until 1817.

1734 Toby dies. By the terms of his will, the land is bequeathed to Timothy Wooster, Peter Johnson, Ebenezer Johnson and Timothy Johnson. All but Wooster are the sons of Ebenezer Johnson, his former master.

1741 Oxford Parish (north farmers of Derby) forms its organization after much opposition from its mother parish of Derby.

1762 Bethany Parish is formed out of Woodbridge Parish.

1763 Benajah Johnson lives in the Skokorat area (Seymour). A daughter, Zeviah, born in 1739, marries Abiel Fairchild and settles a mile northwest of Pinesbridge. Nearer Pinesbridge, on the Lopus Plains, the first settlers are Zadoc Sanford and Hezekiah Clark. Clark is the ancestor of Sheldon Clark, the benefactor of Yale College, and left a bequest for the maintenance of Pinesbridge. In the Nyumph section, Samuel Wheeler builds what is likely the first house. His brothers, Moses, David and James, also settle there. Simeon lives closer to Rimmon. They are the sons of Captain James Wheeler, who lived on Turkey Hill in Derby. Other settlers in the Nyumph section are David French and other members of that family.

April 13: Benajah Johnson dies, age fifty-nine. Johnson appears to be the last person whose remains were carried by litter to the old burying grounds in Derby.

1768 The oldest cemetery in town, sometimes called the "Indian Burial Grounds," is located on a bluff on the west side of the Naugatuck River south of the present Pinesbridge Cemetery. Record of burials:

1768 *Susan, wife of Lieutenant Thomas Clark, died April 11, 1768, age 29.*
1773 *Mrs. Sarah, relative of Benajah Johnson, died May 7, age 72.*
1777 *Pheobe, wife of David Johnson, died August 6, age 47.*
1791 *March 19, Joseph Riggs, age 38, who was a pattern of industry, a friend of virtue and a pillar of society.*
1794 *March 27, Joseph Riggs, son of Joseph and Mistress Ann Riggs, age 8.*
March 24, David Johnson Riggs, son of Joseph and Ann Riggs, age 15.
1797 *Thomas Clark, died October 11, age 33.*

The last burial is for Shubail, the son of Pero, a pureblooded African, and an Indian woman. When it was proposed to bury his remains in the new cemetery on the east side of the river, it was determined that no American Indian would be buried there, so Shubail was taken to the old grounds. For that reason, it became known as the Indian Burial Grounds.

1773 May 7: Sarah Ludlow Brewster Johnson, widow of Benajah Johnson, dies at the home of her daughter, Zeviah Fairchild; her remains are interred in a new burying ground that had been established about five years prior to her death (Indian Burial Grounds). She was a descendant of Roger Ludlow and the Elder William Brewster, early colonial families in this country.

1779 The first demand is made for a division of school districts in the town of old Derby when a district was formed in the extreme northwest part of town, in what is now Beacon Falls, west of the Naugatuck River. This is known as the Rimmon District.

1792 John Allen Coe is born. He would run the first tannery in Beacon Falls, located on the small brook that later became known as Clark's

Brook, which flows into the lands of the Uniroyal Company off Burton Road.

1795 Oxford Turnpike is extended and now follows Route 67, turns northeast to Pinesbridge, crosses the Naugatuck River sixteen times and joins the Naugatuck and New Haven Turnpike at Beacon Brook.

1798 Oxford is incorporated out of the town of Derby.

THE 1800S

1800 Alexander Johnson picks the site of the present cemetery, although some burials were completed prior to this date.

1807 April 13: The early townspeople of Oxford oppose the development of a bridge in the Pinesbridge area, voting to send Abel Wheeler as representative to oppose "any petition that may be brought to the General Assembly to be holden at Hartford in May next praying for the privilege of collecting a toll on Pinesbridge." This begins a long struggle between the Town Meeting voters and the highway firm. It would be resolved twenty years later.

1813 The Methodist Society of Pinesbridge organizes as early as 1813 and possibly earlier. It did not construct the first building until 1846, having earlier met in private homes. The church would move to South Main Street in 1859 and then to its present site on Wolfe Avenue in 1871 (now the United Church of Beacon Falls).

1815 John Coe is born on August 18. He is the son of John Allen Coe. He learns the tanning business from his father and would run the family business until 1850.

1817 Alexander Johnson dies at the age of eighty-seven.

1824 Pinesbridge Turnpike Co. Inc. operates from Waterbury more or less along Chestnut Tree Road as far as the Water Company road and then to Pinesbridge Road, where it joins the Oxford Turnpike.

1827 Clarks Pinesbridge Fund. Sheldon Clark agrees to place a deposit of 100 pounds in money for the Town of Oxford, with the town being allowed to draw interest on the fund to be used for the maintenance of the bridge. "If prudently and fortunately engaged the interest after 12 years will probably build and keep in repair all the bridges that will be ever wanted in that place," notes Clark. The offer is accepted, and the Pinesbridge bridge is constructed in the area that later became part of Beacon Falls.

1830 Rimmon School is built. This building still stands, even though it may not be the same building that was listed as a school in Oxford District Six, recorded in about 1779. It is still on the same location.

1832 Bethany is incorporated.

1833 Milo Lewis maintains a cotton factory in Cotton Hollow. Power is derived from water at the mouth of Beacon Hill Brook to turn the spindles. It is a two-story red-painted factory topped by a bell tower; at 6:00 a.m., the bell is sounded, beginning the long day's work. The mill would be destroyed by fire. Lewis boarded his help in the neighborhood, with rates set for women at $1.25 and for men at $1.50 or $1.75 per week.

1835 A wooden bridge is built about three hundred feet below the present bridge at the Rock Cut by funds furnished by Oxford and Bethany.

1836 Pinesbridge Turnpike Company ceases operation.

The possibility of improving the power of the Naugatuck River is considered. William De Forest secures the privileges at the natural falls below Beacon Hill. Being financially embarrassed, William De Forest removes his proposal and nothing is accomplished.

1838 Julius Curtiss Coe is born on August 3, the sixth generation of the Coe family to carry on the tannery business. He would be the first town clerk and treasurer of Beacon Falls.

1841 Milo Lewis arranges formal agreement with Joel Andrus to help in the cotton factory:

> *This agreement made and intend into this 5th day of Feb. 1841 between Joel Andrus on the first part and Milo Lewis on the second part witnesseth—*

That said Andrus agrees on his part to work for said Lewis in his cotton mill two years from the first day of April 1841 to first day of April 1843. Said Andrus agrees to tend the Picken and take care of the Picking Room in said Lewis Mill as directed by SD Lewis or his overseer. Said Andrus is to conduct himself in a gentlemanly manner toward SD Lewis and his overseer and all persons in any way connected with the Cotton Mill and is to perform all his duties faithfully especially the oiling of any part of the gear or machinery that may be committed to his care. Is to study to make himself useful to his employer by an attentive diligent habit of business and endeavor to excel in the department of Picking. Also SD Andrus agrees to ring the bell and make the fires for the space of time above mentioned at such times as the Regulations of the Mill requires. Further SD Andrus agrees to use his influence in favor of said Mill and the maintenance of all the Rules and use influence to promote the same course of conduct in others committed with SD Mill and also to pay a Respectful Regard to the Sabbath by habitual attendance in some place of public worship. SD Andrus also agrees that in case the business should make it necessary he will quit the picking room for some other department of the business that may be assigned him by SD Lewis or his overseer, and should it so happen that SD Lewis should be obliged to stop his work at the Mill on account of misfortune or hard times this contract is to be null and void—.

SD Lewis on his second part agrees to pay to SD Andrus for the faithful performance of all the duties as above described for the space of two years from the first day of 1841 the sum of nine dollars a month—Eight dollars a month for the first year from April 1st, 1841 to April 1st, 1842 and Ten dollars a month for the second year from April 1st 1842 to April 1st, 1843.

Signed day and date as above as witness our hands for:

Milo Lewis
Sam'l J. Lewis
Joel Andrus

1843 Thomas Sanford invents the friction match.

1844 John Allen Coe is born, son of John and Mary (Hoadley) Coe. John Coe, who was in the tannery business, operated a tannery first in Waterbury and then later at the location of mill complex in Beacon Falls.

Oxford gives up to the new town of Naugatuck a tract of land lying west of the Naugatuck River down to Spruce Brook (High Rock).

1846 First Methodist Episcopal church is built in Pinesbridge through the efforts of John Coe and others. Miles Culver purchases land adjacent to the church and lays out the greater part of the present cemetery into burial lots, which are offered for sale. He transfers the property right of the unsold lots to his son, A.V. Culver, who would later sell to William Gillette.

1847 Elijah Johnson, son of Alexander, occupies his father's homestead until his death at the age of seventy-five.

1849 Naugatuck Railroad is completed from Bridgeport to Waterbury.

May 17: The *Derby Journal* reports that the freight train "Down" was turning a curve about a mile and a half this side of Naugatuck (High Rock). The locomotive suddenly came upon a large cow, which threw the engine off the track, down an embankment about thirty feet into the river, killing the fireman and severely bruising the engineer. The locomotive and the baggage car were so much injured that they probably will be of no further use.

1850 Seymour is incorporated out of Derby.

John Coe Tannery sells land to the American Hard Rubber Company on Main Street and moves to a new site on Lebanon Brook. American Hard Rubber Company builds a dam on the Naugatuck River below High Rock and a three-fourth-mile canal to the factory for water power. D.N. Ropes, William De Forest, G.D. Abbott and John S.C. Abbott are instrumental in the project.

Oxford records show that a lease for a copper mine was made out from a man named Riggs to two men, Coit and Post, conveying mineral rights, which provides one-seventh of the revenue to be paid to Riggs. There is no record of any action under the lease. The 1868 map shows it to be on the Mendlesohn property in Pinesbridge.

1852 Beacon Dam Company is incorporated.

1854 A small portion of Oxford is given to Seymour.

1855 Miss Frances E. Wheeler of Southbury teaches at the Sixth School District of Oxford, Pinesbridge Rimmon School.

A flood destroys the wooden bridge at the Rock Cut.

1856 John Coe, who had moved to New Haven, returns and begins operation of the tannery on Lebanon Brook, manufacturing leather belts and laces; he would be succeeded by his sons, Julius and John Allen.

A new covered bridge is built about three hundred feet north by plans of the American Hard Rubber Company, of which D.N. Ropes is secretary. It is considered the peak of modernism. The three- and four-ton timbers came from local sawmills.

1858 Beacon Dam Company changes its name to the American Hard Rubber Company. Methodist church services are held in Noble Allen's home on Bethany Road and in one of rooms at the Coe Tannery.

1859 The Methodist church congregation moves to a new building on Main Street (Legion Home). The original old building in Pinesbridge would eventually be moved up to Burton Road near the Center School, to be used as a home.

1860 Miss Fannie Coe, daughter of Mr. John Coe, marries Reverend Bennett T. Abbott in the Methodist church on Main Street (former Legion Home and currently Beacon Falls Pizza).

The American Hard Rubber Company moves to College Point, Long Island, and for almost three years the town is nearly deserted.

1861 Mrs. Sarah Wood moves from Lowell, Massachusetts, to Beacon Falls in response to an offer made by the Home Woolen Company in its search for a competent manager for a men's boardinghouse. As she is an earnest church worker and has a piano, her home becomes a center for the social activities of the church.

National Magazine writes that the small cluster of houses and the large manufacturing establishment known as Beacon Falls Station are most picturesquely situated in the midst of some of the wildest scenery of this portion of Connecticut. A great variety of products is manufactured here. Skilled German craftsmen settled in Beacon Falls long before its incorporation.

1863 The Home Woolen Company, a Hartford Corporation, takes over the factory buildings under the supervision of John Wolfe, agent for the Home Woolen Company in Beacon Falls. The purchase consisted of water privileges; a factory three stories high, sixty feet long; thirty houses; and considerable land. A gasworks is erected. Eight sets of machinery are installed, and forty thousand yards of cloth are turned out in a month.

1864 Home Woolen Company increases its capacity and starts manufacturing woolen shawls.

1865 Mr. John Wolfe of the Home Woolen Company and a committee from Bethany—namely Mr. Jason W. Bradley, D.N. Clark and Edwin Pardee—meet on September 26 to discuss the payment of the covered bridge. A payment is made on October 2 from funds provided by the Home Woolen Company and the Town of Bethany.

The name Beacon Falls appears in the acts of the state legislature.

1866 The Unions of Beacon Falls baseball team is organized. Civil War soldiers returning home popularized baseball, a sport played in the camps of both armies.

1867 The Home Woolen Company is enlarged to double its size.

March 7: Ladies Aid Society of the Methodist church is organized by fifteen women at the home of Mrs. J.A. Coe. Mrs. S.A. Wood is elected president and Mrs. Coe, secretary.

March 18: First meeting of the Ladies Aid is held at the home of President S.A. Wood.

1868 Naugatuck Railroad builds a passenger station in Beacon Falls. Mr. Julius Hart is the first agent.

1869 Rock Rimmon Lodge No. 84 (IOOF) is formed. Mr. Riggs in the Sixth District has an ease and method of teaching that will eventually rank him among the foremost of that profession.

1870 Population of Beacon Falls is now 400. The Main Mill is now 330 feet long, 60 and 64 feet wide, three and a half stories and built of brick. There are 5,460 spindles and 70 looms. Nearly thirteen thousand shawls per month are manufactured by skilled workmen.

1871: A TOWN IS BORN

1871 The United Church is built in a grove of pine trees on Wolfe Avenue by land donated by the Home Woolen Co. The first Town Meeting is warned by Buel Buckingham, June 28, at Beechers Hall.

June 1: John Wolfe and others petition the Assembly for creation of a new town.

June 30: Charter of the town is approved. The town is formed out of parts of Oxford, Naugatuck, Bethany and Seymour. The Clarks Pinesbridge Fund is put into the hands of the Town of Beacon Falls. The Pinesbridge Cemetery is turned over to the town. The covered bridge becomes the responsibility of the town.

Record of Town Meeting held July 3, 1871:

Meeting called to order by Mr. Buell Buckingham, warning read. Julius C. Coe appointed Clerk pro tem and sworn in by Justice Patrick Egan. Charter of Town of Beacon Falls, as approved June 30 1871, read by the Clerk and accepted by meeting unanimously.

Voted.

That all necessary officers be elected by acclamation except the Selectmen, Town Clerk, Register of Voters and School Visitors.

That Mr. E.G. Libbey be appointed to assist the Chairman in tending the ballot boxes.

For Town Treasurer—J.C. Coe.
For Constable—H.B. Perry
For Constable—R.H. Griffing, Sr.
For Constable—Harris F. Osborne
For Constable—Andrew Culver
For Grand Juror—Buell Buckingham
For Grand Juror—John French
For Grand Juror—John Wolfe

For Grand Juror—Albert D. Carrington
For Assessor—Herbert Baldwin
For Assessor—Lucius Osborne
For Board of Relief—George A. Twitchell
For Board of Relief—Eben G. Libbey
For Board of Relief—Anson B. Rice
For Register of Births, and Marriages—Charles H. Lounsbury
For Auditor—John A. Coe, Buell Buckingham
Voted Weighter and Sealer of Weights and Measures—J.E. Johnson
For Measures of Wood and Coal—J.E. Johnson, H.B. Perry, John A. Coe
Pound Keepers—Noyes Wheeler, Stiles Clark, James L. Wheeler, Andrew W. Culver, Sidney Baldwin
That each of the Selectmen be appointed Town Agent
For Haywards—M.J. Munson, Lucius Sackett, Almon Switzer
That the collection of Taxes be given to the lowest bidder
For Constable—Almon L. Switzer
Fence Viewers—George A. Twitchell, H.C. Baldwin, Stiles Clark, Ransom Lounsbury
That George A. Twitchell act as auctioneer in giving out the collection of taxes.
That the collection of taxes be struck off to George A. Twitchell at one per cent, that being the lowest bid.
That when this meeting adjourns it to be the first Monday in August 1871 at seven and one half o'clock PM.
H.B. Perry, R.H. Griffing, Almon Switzer, Harris Osborne took the oath of Constable before Patrick Egan, Justice of Peace. Buell Buckingham and John Wolfe took the oath of Grand Juror before Justice Egan. George A. Twitchell, Ransom Lounsbury and H.C. Baldwin took the oath of Fence Viewers before Justice Egan. Ballot Boxes were closed at 5 o'clock p.m. and the Moderator declared the results of the vote as follows:

For Selectman:
Stiles Clark, 85 votes
James Wheeler, 86 votes
Noyes Wheeler, 84 votes
For Town Clerk:
Julius C. Coe, 76 votes
Registers:
H.B. Perry, 43 votes
Patrick Egan, 36 votes

School Visitors:
J.E. Johnson, 48 votes
C.G. Clark, 49 votes
Wheeler, 49 votes

All the above officers were declared elected by the moderator and J.C. Coe was sworn as Town Clerk by Justice Egan.

Meeting adjourned.
Attest: J.C. COE, CLERK

Beacon Falls was so named from Beacon Hill (named by the English) and from which a small but beautiful waterfall descended. There was some opposition to that name by people who wanted it to be called "Home," after the Home Woolen Company Mill.

July 3: Town Meeting is held to elect the first officers of the town; party affiliations are not a factor.

October: Taxable list of the town: $70,392 (from Naugatuck, $11,073; Seymour, $6,000; and Oxford, $53,319)

August 7: The Town of Beacon Falls votes to levy a 2 mill tax for county purposes, to borrow money to pay current expenses and to insure the bridge at the railway depot and paint the same.

July 5: First child born in Beacon Falls is a girl, daughter of Neal and Mary McLaughlin.

September 25: First marriage of a Beacon Falls couple after incorporation of the town of Beacon Falls in Naugatuck: William Simmons and Miss Mary Ann Ashton.

July 21: First boy is born, to William and Mary Shortell.

November 1: The first wedding in Beacon Falls was performed by Reverend J. Chittendon of Waterbury: Thomas Bamford and Anna Simmons.

1872 Patrick Egan is appointed a "Taverner."

Reverend Eldrige Lounsbury is pastor of United Church.

Dedication of United Church is held.

Beacon Falls receives $1,748.25 from Town Deposit Fund as its share from Bethany, Oxford, Naugatuck and Seymour. This fund was derived from the sale of western lands (Western Reserve).

1873 Town Report, 1872–73:

> *Members of School Committee:*
> *Center School—John Coe*
> *Nyumph School—David French*
> *Rimmon School—Andrew Culver*
> *Expenses of Schools—$1,031.17. The State contributed $350.00. There is no record when Center School was built but, as the earliest school records extend back to 1864 there evidently were school privileges before then.*

1874 A bridge is built at the Nyumph School on Bethany Road for thirty-two dollars.

The Good Will Lodge of Good Templars has a flourishing existence.

Knights of Pythians hall is dedicated.

1876 High Rock Grove is noted as a pleasure resort. The Naugatuck Railroad provides a station, and the place is patronized by many sightseers and picnickers, who enjoy two spacious pavilions and other houses, a croquet field, a merry-go-round, a skating rink and boats for rowing on the river.

Home Woolen Company suspends operation.

September issue of *Seymour Record*: "The Home Woolen Company is pushing the repairs of their Dam as fast as possible. They are doing it in such a manner that it must be substantial….Our enterprising Townsman, Thomas Sloane, is putting up a building on Main Street (Rock House), near the residence of Patrick Egan, Esq. for a barber shop."

1877 Julius Coe is elected to Connecticut House of Representatives.

Town Meeting is held to vote on allowing the Selectmen to give licenses for the sale of intoxicating beverages. The residents narrowly reject the proposal, and Beacon Falls becomes a "dry town" in September.

October: A special meeting of a petition of residents is held. The petition claims that one of the persons voting at the previous meeting had voted "No" when he meant to vote "Yes." The individual made a public statement that the reason for his mistake was that he could not read. The meeting is held, and the residents vote that the Selectmen be empowered to grant licenses, making the sale of liquor legal. Following the meeting, the Selectmen receive a request from a woman that local taverns be forbidden to serve her husband because he was a terrible drunkard. The Selectmen notify the taverns that sales to the individual would cause the taverns to lose their license.

1878 Julius Coe moves to New Haven and sets up wholesale leather business. His brother John Allen Coe maintains the tannery business here.

1879 John Wolfe becomes owner of some of the machinery, thirty tenements and two hundred acres of land of the previously owned Home Woolen Company.

1880 Home Woolen Company is reorganized. Nearly $500,000 is expended. Eighteen sets of machinery are set in motion, and three hundred hands are employed.

Population of the town is 379.
Reverend William Rogers becomes minister of United Church.

The Beacon Mill and Power Company receives a carload of shingles from Michigan and will repair its tenements and put them in order for renting.

Noyes Wheeler kills a black snake in his pasture measuring six feet, eight inches.

Beacon Falls Tennis Club is formed.

1882 Reverend J.J. Moffitt is the new minister at United Church.

John Allen Coe and John Bronson of Waterbury exchange properties, with Bronson taking over the Coe property on South Main Street and the Coes taking over in Waterbury. John Bronson operates a brass novelty business.

1883 Reverend A.S. Hagerty, next minister of United Church, marries Miss Leila Bronson, daughter of Mr. John Bronson.

Mortgage is paid off at the United Church.

A steel bridge is built at Pinesbridge.

Pinesbridge Cemetery is enlarged and plotted in blocks under the direction of John W. Rogers, David T. Sanford and Charles Botsford.

1884 The novelty business of John Bronson is taken over by his three sons, Homer, George and Luther. At this time, the name is changed to the Homer D. Bronson Company. They manufacture artwork in brass and copper.

John Wolfe of the Home Woolen Company retires and is succeeded by Clarence J. Bodfish.

November 4: Republicans are elected to the Connecticut General Assembly, this being the election where party affiliations were recorded for judge of probate and state representative. No party affiliations for other offices of the town are recorded.

Republicans meet at the German clubroom (Church Street) for the purpose of organizing a Blaine and Logan club. The club will raise a banner soon and probably will invite some parties to give them address of the occasion.

The Beacon Falls Drum Corps is organized under the instruction of F.W. Mills. They have all new equipment, one bass and nine snare drums, and are making a fine appearance on the street.

The Blaine and Logan club has received about fifty members since its organization began. It expects to get suits and rigs for dress parade soon. There will be a fine display on the field.

The young men of town organize a literary association and will meet in the building known as the old Shoemaker's Shop.

H.C. Baldwin of Naugatuck delivers an address at Brown's Hall and organizes a Butler and West club of eight members with the hopes of more. They have a large attendance.

The Beacon Falls Drum Corps attends the Woodbridge Fair in the team of Andrew Culver, which is finely decorated.

1885 The Novelty Rubber Company is formed, manufacturing rubber buttons.

Homer D. Bronson Company makes more additions to its factory.

Beacon Falls becomes a mission of St. Augustine's Church of Seymour. There are about one hundred Catholics in town. The first Mass is said in a private home on Main Street, delivered by the pastor of St. Augustine's Church, Reverend Richard Gragan.

Town Meeting: Brown's Hall is rented for another year.

A 10 mill tax is levied on grand list.

It is voted to erect tombstones, not to exceed $100, on graves of Joseph and Julia Riggs.

The pleasant Sundays find many people walking to High Rock Grove and no doubt happy to see the picnic season approaching.

Mr. Otto Seiler leases the property of Mrs. H. Schweig. He proposes to bottle lager besides doing regular hotel business. Advertisement:

> *Substantial Mill and best water power in the Naugatuck Valley for sale at Beacon Falls Connecticut with or without woolen machinery; Dam and land superior. Mill building 330 by 50 feet, four floors and basement.*

> *The rooms are high and well lighted and suited for almost any kind of manufacturing that requires upper floors. Only 2 or 3 hours from New York. The real estate and machinery will be sold in lots to suit purchasers. Mill, 165 by 50 feet, four stories and basement will be sold separate if desired. For further particulars inquire of Beach and Company, 211 State, Hartford, Connecticut.*

Much indignation is expressed by many persons here respecting an article that lately appeared in a neighboring journal attacking rather severely the editor of the *Seymour Record*. Never mind, friend Sharpe, you have the respect of all by treating this as all other such articles, viz.: with silent contempt. The barking of curs does not injure, and mud thrown by boys will usually stick to the fingers more than to the clothes at whom it is cast.

The personal property of the estate of the late Julia E. Riggs will be sold at auction at her late residence near Pinesbridge on Wednesday, September 17, at one o'clock; also the material of the old bridge.

George Clark cut his knee rather severely with an axe. He met a similar misfortune a year ago.

A short time ago, a man from Naugatuck drove off the main road leading to Beacon Falls and nigh immersed himself into the Home Woolen Mill Company canal. He was badly broken up and thinks that someone should pay him for his misfortune.

A boy who had been living in the family of William Smythe suddenly disappeared and with him about thirty dollars in money. Officers were sent in pursuit, but at last accounts he had not been found.

At the Town Meeting held at Brown's Hall, the selectmen's report was received and fund received and accepted, also the treasurer's and school visitors' reports and the one on the town deposit. On the cemetery at Pinesbridge, a committee reported expenses for enlarging and repairing the same: $653. Accepted. William D. Gillette was appointed sexton to take charge of the cemetery and sell lots and also John W. Rogers, C.D. Bodfish and D.T. Sanford were appointed to establish price of lots and complete a map of the same.

There seems to be some doubt by some of the newspaper report about Rogers and his rattlesnake at High Rock Grove, and yet it is true to the main. He caught the rattler by placing a stick on its neck and then seizing it just back of the head with his hand; he then placed the dangerous reptile in a cigar box and exhibited it about the grove. Know only this, but he removed the reptile from one box to another and handled it with such freedom as to make people shudder for his chances. There were many Waterbury witnesses of the lad's foolhardiness or daring, but the snake was not much over two feet long.

October: Special Town Meeting is held to hire someone to prosecute those people violating the law against trotting horses over the bridge. Idea rejected. Instead, it is decided to pay a reward of one dollar to any person entering a complaint that led to the conviction for the crime.

1886 The correspondent and agent for the *Record* in Beacon Falls is Miss Ella E. Wood, who is authorized to receive subscriptions, and those who can conveniently do so are requested to notify her of occurrences about town.

V.H. McEwen of Naugatuck opens a meat market, and Arthur Curtiss of Ansonia has charge of it.

Messrs. Terrill and Bacon report their trade to be improving and look for a good spring and summer trade.

It has been a long time since our schools were in as good condition as now. The Misses Elwell and Twitchell are proving themselves fully capable of ensuring order and imparting knowledge.

The Drum Corps hires Clark's Hall for the winter evenings and appoints their several committees for various objects.

Last Thursday night, as William Titley was getting off the night freight, he fell, striking upon his head and right side. He was picked up insensible and taken to his home but did not recover consciousness until the following day. He is somewhat better now. Doctor F.B. Tuttle of Naugatuck attends him.

Beacon Falls Rifle Club is formed. It is to practice every Saturday afternoon.

The Homer D. Bronson begins the manufacture of bronze piano panels and long continuous hinges.

A High Rock scene decorates the curtain of the new Jacques Theater in Waterbury, which opened on November 1.

Mr. Edward Gruber, a young man, applies at the Emery J. Terrill store on Main Street for a job as a clerk because he is anxious to learn the business and someday hopes to own the business.

Bronson-Brown, prominent families in Beacon Falls, announce a marriage. One of those happy events in which people are so much interested took place on Thursday afternoon at the residence of Mr. and Mrs. Ezekial Brown, resulting in the marriage of their daughter, Miss Maria Brown, to George Bronson, both of Beacon Falls. They were married by the Reverend W.C. Roberts of Ansonia, with Episcopal ceremonies. The bride was dressed in grosgrain blue silk, while the bridesmaid, Miss Maria L. Barnett of Ansonia, wore a white cashmere trimmed with brocaded velvet. George Griswold of Waterbury acted as groomsman. After the marriage ceremony was performed and the couple made man and wife, and congratulations and wishes for prosperity and happiness were given, all were invited to a table heavily loaded with good things, turkey and other meats, a great abundance and variety of cake, fruit in variety etc., which was evidently appreciated by the guests, and all were satisfied that Mr. and Mrs. Brown were equal to the occasion. Among the relatives present on Mr. Bronson's side were Mr. and Mrs. John Bronson and their daughter, Lila; Mr. and Mrs. Homer Bronson and daughter Helen; and Mr. and Mrs. Luther Bronson and son Frank. Relatives on Mrs. Brown's side included Mr. and Mrs. Alfred Barnett and daughters Melvina and Maria; Mrs. George Brown and daughter Alice; and Mrs. Selby, all of Ansonia; also William Brown and son Thomas of Providence, Rhode Island. Also as invited guests, Mr. G.H. Griswold of Waterbury and Miss Ella E. Wood of Beacon Falls. Mrs. Jerome Munson assisted on the occasion Mr. Norton of Waterbury was down with his hack, carrying relatives from and to their residences and to the depot. Three elegant bride's cakes were made by Meigs and Trott of Waterbury, one of them being a pyramid of three cakes, while on top an archway, in the center of which was stood an angel with a hammer striking against two harps. The presents were numerous and useful. In the evening Mr. and Mrs. Bronson were serenaded by the Beacon Falls Silver Drum Corps, and a dance given with a general invitation through the town. Thus ended a happy and pleasant entertainment long to be remembered. Mr. and Mrs. Bronson will board for the present with Mr. John Bronson.

Mr. and Mrs. George T. Clark, who were lately married, seem to be supremely happy in their new home. We wish for them many pleasant and prosperous years.

1887 Mrs. David Clark, age fifty-six years, dies at her residence at a quarter past midnight. She had been sick some time, and the death messenger has called her to rest. She was respected by all and kind to all and especially to the poor, caring for their comfort. She had long been a member of the ladies' sewing society, and the ladies of that society, assisted by a few friends, purchased a handsome cross of white flowers, based with pansies and other flowers, for the funeral, as a token of their sympathy and esteem. The funeral services were held at her late residence at 1:00 p.m. and at the church 2:00 p.m. on Wednesday afternoon, conducted by the Reverend Mr. Smith of Naugatuck. She leaves a son and family to mourn her loss. Burial at Pinesbridge Cemetery. The pallbearers were Jerome Hubbell, George Twitchell, John Bradley and Gregory Monroe. The family return thanks for expressions and tokens of sympathy so freely extended. Newspaper report of memorial services held in Seymour, Connecticut:

> *The showers of Sunday night settled the dust and then the clouds sped away leaving but their teardrops as a blessing to earth. The day dawned and the arrangements were completed without hindrance. On the arrival of the Beacon Falls Silver Drum Corps by the train a little after two, the Veterans, preceded by the Silver Drum Corps, marched to the engine house, where the Citizens Fire Company awaited them.*
>
> *The line of march was taken to the cemetery, where the G.A.R. service and the decoration of graves of deceased soldiers took place, after which the line formed in reverse order and the procession returned and marched up Main Street to Bank Street and down Second Street to the Opera House.*

The meeting was called to order by H.S. Chamberlain, P.C. of Upson Post and opened with a selection by the Tingue Mfg. band. The divine blessing was invoked by T.S. Ladd. The following poem was then read by S.Y. Beach, Esq., in a distinct and impressive manner.

Two pair of frozen ears and one frostbitten nose are reported as the result of the recent cold spell.

The number of militia enrolled last year was sixty-eight. The number assessed two dollars is fifty-three.

The Misses Elwell and Twitchell, our schoolteachers, are very popular and doing excellent work.

Julius Hart, collector of taxes for the town of Beacon Falls, receives the rate book for 1886 and will be at the Town Clerk's Office on the first day of March.

Reverend A.S. Hagerty preaches an excellent sermon on "Christian Steadfastness," taking for his text the words found in Hebrews 10:38, 39.

C.J. Bodfish, agent of the Home Woolen Mill Co., purchases a large truck horse weighing about 1,300 pounds for its work, doing away with oxen and making their expenses lighter.

Antiquarians are a rarity here; yet in a private library are found several books of ancient date, among the number one printed in 1680 that has been the property of the ancestors of its present owner.

Thomas West resigns the position of overseer of the weave room of the Home Woolen Mill Co. and goes to Meriden to take a position of superintendent.

Thomas J. Hall of Schaghticoke, New York, accepts the position as overseer of the weave room.

The Beacon Falls Silver Drum Corps gives an oyster supper at the Methodist Episcopal church on February 19. Tickets are sold for chances on a silver castor, a barrel of flour, one hundred cigars and case, one-half cord of wood and dozen cabinet pictures taken by the committee of arrangements, Thomas Lewis, Frank Reffelt and David Byars. Any fancy articles received by the committee are cheerfully accepted. Proceeds for their new uniforms. Admission ten cents, supper twenty-five cents, children fifteen cents. A toolbox will be given to one of the three loom fixers receiving the most votes, namely A. Hirsch, J. Gerry or A. Walker.

Messrs. Terrill and Bacon conclude to do away with giving credit and will hereafter conduct their business on the cash system.

The meat market under the name of V.H. McEwen of Naugatuck presents an inviting appearance and under the efficient management of their genial clerk, Arthur Curtiss, bids fair to be freely patronized.

John Lapraik, the new overseer of the Home Woolen Mill Co. works, resigns.

Those who own dogs are generally up to the mark, a large number having been registered.

The agent of the Berlin Bridge Company comes to town to make arrangements for the new bridge at Pinesbridge, which is to be completed as soon as possible.

Mr. C.L. Hathaway of Adams, Massachusetts, lately overseer of the dressing room of the Home Woolen Mill Co., resigns. He was also of service to the church. William Hoffman of this place takes charge of the room.

The Home Woolen Mills Company concludes to change hours of work from 6:45 a.m. and out at 6:15 p.m.; closing on Saturdays at a quarter to 1:00 p.m. and having the afternoon. It will also pay weekly instead of monthly.

A game of baseball is played by the Wide-a-Wakes and the German Giants. Following is the score: German Giants: 3-1-4-6-2-0-0-2-10—28; Wide-a-Wakes: 1-0-2-0-1-0-0-3-0—7. A victory for the German Giants.

Home Woolen Company builds more house on Main Street.

The Hothouse of Wales Sackett presents a very attractive appearance.

D.J. Carrington has a large quantity of potatoes of very fine quality that he is offering for sale.

It is a stubborn fact that more than two-thirds of the farms in town are mortgaged, and still they vote to continue the system that makes them a servant of usury to the bankers.

The Civil Authority's meeting is held at Bronson's Hall as required by the statute for the purpose of selecting jurors for one year as follows: Herbert Baldwin, Cornelius Munson, Charles Lewis, George S. Baldwin, David Carrington, John Wolfe, Olin D. Buckingham, David T. Sanford, Jerome Andrews, Homer D. Bronson, Charles B. Clark, Sheldon Clark, Noyes Wheeler, Jerome B. Hubbell, David M. French and Ransom Lounsbury.

S.M. Burns, boss carpenter, of the Naugatuck Railroad, makes a decided improvement at the passenger station by putting up a new platform. It is understood that Superintendent Beach is to send several loads of dirt to grade around the station, which is much needed. F.W. Mills and Herman Kupke have the pleasure of an increase in their fireside group. May they well exclaim the poet, "It's nice to be the father of a bouncing baby boy."

The mason work for the new iron bridge (Pinesbridge) is nearly ready, which is soon to be put on foundation.

One of our public benefactors, Daniel J. Carrington, commences his usual vacation by distributing ice about the village.

The town clerk reports that an unusual number of dogs have been registered. Perhaps the rumor that was afloat to the effect that one of our constables was soon to make an onslaught on dogs caused vigorous action on the part of the taxpayers.

Ezekial Brown, proprietor of the High Rock House, purchases a narrow strip of land from the Home Woolen Mill Company to enlarge his driveway on the north side of the hotel.

George Wheeler, formerly a butcher here, now of Goddard and Fowler of Naugatuck, drives into town twice a week with its meat cart.

The Home Woolen Mill Company shuts down about July 1 for an indefinite period, and in consequence, about three hundred hands are thrown out of employment. Quite a number of its employees obtained work in adjoining towns and go to and from their work by cars, and others moved away. There are many rumors about, as there always is in such cases, but the truth is past finding out. There is one fact apparent, that for the fine class of goods that they are making there is a drought in the market.

The Classic Reading Club sells all its personal effects, which belonged to the club room, at public auction.

The Beacon Falls Silver Drum Corps meets for the last time to disband, sells all of furniture and will place on sale all of its drum corps suits.

Center School District No. 1 holds its annual meeting:

> *The first quarterly conference is held at the Methodist Episcopal church. The Reverend W. Wadell, presiding elder, is in the chair. It is expected the Reverend E.R. Foley will be retained here as long he can be paid. It is hoped that all who remain in town will aid the church by their presence as well as money, that it is not necessary to close the church.*
>
> *Andrew Culver brings the price of milk down to the bounds of reason, and he deserves the support of the people in his efforts to break the milk monopoly. There is no reason why milk should sell for more in Beacon Falls than it does in New Haven.*
>
> *Some people thought if Mr. Walker left the village that the* Agitator *would be a dead issue. But they are destined to disappointment, for the news will be written just the same, and if you do a mean action you will see it in print.—Mary B.M.*

1888 A four mill tax increase is assessed on the grand list for the Rimmon School District.

The American Telegraph and Telephone Company has poles for a new line through the town.

"Blizzard of '88." A passenger train stalls for several days between passenger station and High Rock. Expenses for snow removal for the year of 1888 total $143.78.

The Homer D. Bronson Company builds a new boiler room.

Selectmen make repairs to the Butler Bridge (Pinesbridge).

1889 Selectmen call a meeting on January 7 to replace or repair section of wooden bridge in the center of town.

Meeting held on January 9 proves to be a fizzle. Many motions and amendments made, but all are voted down.

Beacon Mill and Power Company of Hartford become owners of Home Woolen Company property.

New London passenger train leaves Beacon Falls at 5:04 p.m. straight through without changing at Milford.

Two thousand men from Company A enjoy a day at High Rock Grove. A concert by Wheeler and Wilson band is given.

The Homer D. Bronson Company purchases a fine-looking gray horse for use in general work.

Beacon Mill and Power Co. lease building to the Standard Woolen Company. The officers are Henry I. Buttry, Fred Kitchen and Clarence J. Bodfish. $18,000, 720 shares at $25 each. C.F. Kimpton in charge of machine work. John Titley, boss carder.

Beacon Falls Mill and Power Co. formed with $58,000, 580 shares at $100. Subscribers:

Beach and Co., Hartford, 359 shares
Charles M. Beach, Trustee West Hartford 120 shares
T.B. Beach, Hartford, 1 share
John S. Camp, Hartford, 100 shares
T.B. Beach, temporary clerk and secretary

Arbor Day is duly observed in the Center School District. Planting of trees in the schoolyard: three maple trees, one chestnut tree, lilac bushes and shrubbery etc.

1890 Several families are making preparations for poultry raising. William Owens believes in early chickens. He has a hen that hatched seven little chicks on Saturday, February 8, and has three more he's setting. Ezekial Brown is building a new barn; William Rich is doing the work. Thomas Donahue is building a stone wall under the building he purchased from the Home Woolen Mill Co. some time ago. He expects to move the building to adjoin the other end and make two nice tenements.

The young men have organized a Young Men's Literary Club and will give a series of dances. The first social dance will be at the German Hall.

Smith Botsford, the veteran fox hunter, and D.J. Carrington, while out fox hunting, capture an eighteen-pound coon and hawk that measures four feet, seven inches from tip to tip.

Mr. C.H. Curtiss discontinues running his meat wagon again.

George Luddington purchases the house and lot known as the Miles place, as well as a tract of land adjoining formerly owned by John French. Mr. Luddington will at once make repairs and go to farming.

George Clark is still erecting four coal pits to be burned. David Boswell will have the care of them. Mr. Clark finds a ready sale for all of his charcoal in Waterbury and commences to deliver it.

C.F. Curtiss purchases the meat interests of Harvey N. Atwood and takes over possession of the market.

Miles and Stahl of Seymour commence driving in town with meat.

Frank Reigel of Seymour comes to town once a week with fish. William Gray of Beacon Falls has gone to work for him.

Who can come to the front and say this town is not growing when we consider the increase of numbers coming in through the business done by the Standard Woolen Co., and the number of teams coming full force to town shows that much food is required to sustain the growing population. Mr. Harvey Atwood, who sold out his business to Mr. C.E. Curtiss, had tried to earn an honest living, but so many bought their meat elsewhere that it cut off the income that properly belonged to the town market, consequently sold out, much to the regret of townspeople here. It is earnestly hoped Mr. Curtiss may be generally patronized and thereby sustain a market in the town.

David Sanford finds a ready sale for his charcoal and is now carrying it to Ansonia Brass and Copper Co.

1891 October: The residents vote 40–10 to abolish the school districts and form a school group.

1892 May 2: A special committee of six members is picked to consolidate the schools. The members are Herbert Baldwin, Homer D. Bronson, Carlos F. Kimpton, Emerson Terrell, Cornelius W. Munson and John H. Baldwin.

The east section of the covered bridge is declared unsafe. A sixty-foot section is replaced with a steel bridge from the east bank to the first river pier.

The Selectmen were H.C. Baldwin, C.W. Munson and O.D. Buckingham.

1893 May 22: A Special Town Meeting is called by the Selectmen to consider admissibility of having a "lock-up" in town.

May 27: At the meeting, the subject is debated heatedly, and several amendments are offered. No agreement is reached, and the entire matter is postponed indefinitely. The outcome of the meeting is considered a defeat for the temperance movement.

Jay Beecher, a carpenter and builder, builds a store and several houses in town and for a short time is engaged in the mercantile business.

The 1893 session of the General Assembly gives women the right to vote in town on school district questions relating to the selection of School District electors.

The following table shows the number of women voting in 1893 and 1894:

Year	Seymour	Oxford	Beacon Falls
1893	5	0	0
1894	1	0	0

1894 April 6: Rock Rimmon Grange, an agricultural society, is established at Clark's Hall, named after the mountains known as Rock Rimmon that lie in the southeastern section of the Town, with twenty-five charter members.

1895 At the Annual Meeting, the town votes to establish the post of truant officer for the purpose of securing a better attendance of scholars at the schools in town. Richard J. Beach is appointed.

Nyumph School is closed. Students are transferred to the Center School.

The Derby–New Haven turnpike ceases operation.

The Connecticut Highway Department is organized.

The Homer D. Bronson Company makes more additions to its factory.

1896 June 29: A rattlesnake is captured at High Rock that measures forty-four and a half inches long, with six rattles; it is brought in by P. Schaffrath and brother and L.S. Chapman of the Storrs Agricultural College.

October 3: Residents vote to appropriate a sum not to exceed $100 to supply the school with free textbooks. The following year, only $50 is allowed for additional books.

October 3: A burial ordinance is passed: "Whenever any burial lot in Pinesbridge shall hereafter be sold, that if such lot not wholly paid for on or before the expiration of 3 months from the date of purchase, the sexton shall, after giving notice to the purchaser thereof, remove the body occupying the lot from there and place it in that portion of the cemetery reserved for the poor, such removal shall be made sometime during the next six months."

1898 A special committee of Homer D. Bronson and George T. Blood is formed to investigate the use of Center School and Pinesbridge School; the cost of the building a picket fence around Center School; and buying a lot north of Center School.

November: Report is made. Residents try to postpone to next October.

The Beacon Falls Rubber Shoe Company is organized under George Lewis and others.

March: The skating rink at High Rock burns to the ground. It is believed to have been set by men of the road who were trying to keep warm.

June: The Naugatuck Railroad rebuilds a new skating rink at High Rock.

1899 At a special Town Meeting, it is voted to purchase a lot next to the school from the Beacon Falls Rubber Shoe Company. It is voted to build a picket fence around the entire area. A total of not more than $2,000 is appropriated. Committee of H.D. Bronson, C. Munson and John Rice is named to supervise the work. A two-story structure with two more rooms, the same size as original structure, is added. Between 1899 and 1904, only three would be rooms used; the fourth would be used as a playroom or for special projects. The fourth room of Center School would be used as a classroom when children from Cotton Hollow who attended Joint School District in Naugatuck were transferred to Center School. These children would be taken back and forth to school by a team of horses.

February: Fire razes all the buildings of the Homer D. Bronson Company.

March 30: First shoes are made in the new factory of the Beacon Falls Rubber Shoe Company. The first ticket for 144 pairs was made, which would grow to 5.5 million by 1920.

May 11: Beacon Hose Company No. 1 is organized in the cutting room of the Beacon Falls Rubber Shoe Company, consisting of twenty men and these officers:

Foreman: George Butz
Asst. Foreman: E.J. Stevens
Secretary: Harry R. Allen
Treasurer: Bradford Wakefield

May 26: Beacon Falls Field Club is organized at the home of Mister Lewis Warner. The object of the club shall be to develop the games of lawn tennis and croquet and promote general sociability, with these officers:

Pres. George Woodsun
Vice Pres. H.D. Warner
Sec. and Treas. Richard Fisher

November: Cornerstone is laid at St. Michael's Church with Father Rigney.

December: The first Mass is held in the new St. Michael's Church on Main Street.

Reverend John Balfour Smith is the new minister of Methodist Church.

The 1900s

1900 Town Health Report: seven cases measles, one case scarlet fever and one case typhoid fever.

March 11: St. Michael's Church, a wooden frame structure with seating capacity for two hundred people, is dedicated.

Center School Teachers:

Primary: Emma Lockwood
Intermediate: Iris Munson
Grammar: Edith Burnett
Rimmon School: Alice Ward

Methodist church changes denomination to be Congregational, and the name is changed to the United Church of Beacon Falls, serving all denominations. Reverend Walton M. Patton, professor at Yale, is the new minister at United Church. United Church is officially incorporated on July 6.

The first marriage in St. Michael's Roman Catholic Church in Beacon Falls, the first Catholic marriage ever solemnized in town, is conducted. The contracting parties are Miss Agnes M. Woodhouse and Charles Curley.

Beacon Lodge No. 28 Knights of Pythias is formed.

1901 Mr. Edward Gruber, with Mr. Grover N. Cook as a partner, purchases the store from Emery L. Terrell, son of the former owner, who had acquired the business at the passing of his father.

1902 May 1: Fair is held by Ladies of St. Michael's Church.

1903 Beacon Falls Schools are placed under State Superintendent DeWitt Allen, who is supervisor of five area towns. Mr. Allen groups the pupils into grades 1 to 8.

Rice Lane, once known as Beacon Hill Road, is discontinued as a road to a point where it intersects the road up the hill to Wilbur Seeley.

Connecticut begins issuing license plates for cars. License plate no. 1207 was the first in Beacon Falls, issued to Homer D. Bronson.

1904 Beacon Falls Rubber Shoe Company suffers a major fire in the office and accounting departments. Fortunately, the records found in the vault are in perfect condition, permitting business to continue without interruption.

April 16: The town builds a new highway, starting at a point near the foot of Munson Hill and ending at the foot of Gillette Hill and running parallel with the old highway (Old Turnpike Road) and halfway between the old highway and the Naugatuck River.

July 19: Work is started on new parsonage for the United Church.

1905 May 3: Selectmen are authorized to meet with the Naugatuck Valley Electric Company in regard to proposed trolley line.

October 5: Selectmen negotiate with Beacon Falls Rubber Shoe Co. for electric lights on Main Street. The town accepts proposal of the concern to provide twelve to fifteen lights for five years. The lights are to be paid for at a rate of twenty-five dollars per light annually.

1906 Trolley service opens from New Haven to Waterbury with half-hour service.

Bart Howell is named foreman of the Beacon Falls Hose Company, succeeding George Butz.

Charles Lovine, the photographer from Naugatuck, takes views of the interior of the Beacon Falls Rubber Shoe Company.

Owing to the high water in the Naugatuck River, about 150 feet of the trestle is washed away.

The engine used in building the abutments for the railroad has been moved across the tracks, and work has begun on the second abutment.

The Whist party given by the Rathbone sisters is a pleasant affair. These parties are given every two weeks and are very much enjoyed by those who attend.

The Alpine Athletic Club celebrates its first anniversary.

Harvey Atwood buys the seventy-eight-acre farm from Sherman Elkins. This is the Feldspar Avenue area. The Mike Carroll house was the original Atwood house, moved from the place where Frank Bronson built his new home on Feldspar Avenue.

The school board votes to extend the grammar school work one year, making a grammar school course of nine years. A child who spends one year more in grammar school work is more mature and better prepared to take up the work of the high school.

School teachers for the school year include:

Grammar: Eva T. Lind
Intermediate: Anna M. Gessler
Second Primary: Alice H. Thall
First Primary: Catherine Fischer
Rimmon: Marion Fowler

1907 Cotton Hollow schoolchildren now travel by trolley.

William (Pop) Lee is named foreman of the Beacon Falls Hose Company. (He served as chief until 1950).

June 2: Memorial services are held in Pinesbridge Cemetery by five old veterans who braved the storm.

New Haven Railroad puts in a second spur of tracks along its line.

1908 The minutes read: "The special Town meeting called for this date was not held on account of NO attendance. Special meeting held to consider sale of a piece of Town Property."

The E. Gruber Company has coal sheds built to which the railroad company is having a spur track laid so that coal can be unloaded from the cars into the sheds.

A new drugstore is built on Bridge Street, Leo F.J. Hoffstadt, Druggist and Chemist. The store accepts all freight by trolley. 276 cases are sent by trolley to its customers in one day.

1909 Reverend Rigney dies. Reverend John A. Sullivan, administrator of parish, is appointed pastor of St. Augustine's Church in Seymour.

1910 Homer D. Bronson Company sells all property and interests to a group of Naugatuck Valley businessmen. The company will still operate under the same name.

Beacon Building Association is formed, with headquarters on Church Street.

1911 High Rock merry-go-round and dance floor burn down. Squaw Rock was a corner of the dance floor. Glass present all around the rock was due to people smashing their bottles on it. The rock originally fell from the top of High Rock.

Reverend Fletcher is the new minister of United Church.

1913 Beacon Falls Rubber Shoe Co. designates a Maltese cross with a notch in a tree as its trademark (Top Notch). This will be its brand name.

1914 The founder of the Beacon Falls Rubber Shoe Company, George Lewis, dies. His son, Tracy Lewis, takes over as president of the Company.

1915 March 15: Motion is made and carried that the tax rate for 1915 on the grand list of 1914 be placed at 17 mills.

Center School is crowded, so the Nyumph School is reopened. Elizabeth Donovan serves as teacher.

A longtime Selectman and representative, Herbert Baldwin, dies. He also was the caretaker of the Pinesbridge Cemetery.

Milton Carrington, pound keeper, has in his possession a stray horse. Advertised—no claimants—horse to be disposed as per state statute.

Town votes to purchase more land for cemetery from William H. Jones, directly back of present cemetery, also same width, and runs back to the fence at the trolley tracks.

October 4: The proposed constitutional amendment concerning mileage to the General Assembly is voted—50 Yes, 12 No.

Election is held: 105 ballots cast: 72 straight Republican; 15 straight Democrat; 12 split; 5 thrown out for improper marking.

Rubber Shoe Company readies plans for building Top Notch Hotel—seventy-five rooms and restaurant to accommodate women needed to work in the plant.

John Bowe and Victor Lingenheld are granted permission to keep open their places of business until twelve o'clock midnight on all such days as they can legally keep open said places of business. This permit will become void at twelve o'clock at night on October 3, 1916, unless revoked for cause.

The government gives two brass cannons to the Town of Beacon Falls. (No record of such is ever found.)

Two-story, two-classroom addition is added to southern part of Center School facing Burton Road.

1916 March 14: Beacon Falls Rubber Shoe Company makes application to place four supporting pillars in the highway

(Burton Road) between the office building and what is known as #1 storeroom for the purpose of supporting a proposed addition to the office building.

Application by J.T. Crowley, superintendent.

March 16: Town Meeting is held for first time upstairs in the new Top Notch Movie House on Main Street.

October 2: The Town of Beacon Falls takes over the care and expenses of the new town park. (where the firehouse is today).

Eight hydrants are installed:

Main Street, Catholic Church
At bridge over canal on Main Street (Gabe's Mobil)
Near John Bowe's property on Main Street (Rock Cut)
Railroad Avenue
Norton's Corner (Bethany Road)
Power House, South Main Street
Vicinity of Center School
Vicinity of Center School

1917 War is declared by the United States.

A seven-year-boy dies after being struck by automobile on Main Street.

1918 Special school instruction classes are held three evenings a week for children who were working but had not completed grammar school. Deprived of religious services in the Pinesbridge area, United Church Sunday School reorganizes using the school district (Rimmon School).

Old-time picnic excursions to one of the New Haven beaches, which in early day was accomplished by wagon, is revived. Three trolley cars are filled with the church and Sunday school excursionists.

First mention of the Boy Scouts of Beacon Falls, with Mr. John Rice as scoutmaster and Mr. Harry J. Lobdell, Mr. Harry Sparks and Mr. John W. Cook as scout committee.

United War Campaign is organized at the request of President Wilson. Connecticut quota, 3,000: L.C. Warner—Beacon Falls Shoe Company; Frank Bronson—Homer D. Bronson Company.

November 11: Armistice is signed.

1919 Americanization classes for non-citizens are instituted.

Reverend Martin O'Brian is the last priest under jurisdiction of Seymour at St. Michael's Church.

Ford fire truck is purchased for the Beacon Hose Company.

Welcome Home parade is held for World War I veterans. Mr. Patrick Malone leads the parade with a white bulldog.

Post No. 25 American Legion is formed.

Many towns are now employing district nurses whose duty it is to look after the health of the children in the schools and to promote better living conditions in the home. The fact that Connecticut led in the number of men rejected for army service proves the need a statewide campaign along the lines of health and sanitation, one that properly must begin in the schools.

September 18: The following are registered as "To be made" voters:

Theodore Braun	Robert L. McCarthy
William Bulka	William F. O'Keefe
Henry W. Burkle	Herman Reyer
Lewis C. Callahan	Paul J. Richter
Martin H. Daley	George Rismiller
Willet Dubois	Anthony Sabia
William B. Evans	Charles A. Seimer
Raymond F. Fruin	Sidney J. Shepard
Wilfred Happy	George W. Simpson
Christian Heiss	Henry Strauber
Frank Keireschke	George Surface
Edward Lafferty	John W. Winch
Rudolph Lafferty	James Woodward
Fred Laville	William Zick

1920 Charles Kevit of the Top Notch baseball team pitches a no-hitter.

Bobby Faulkes, Black world bantamweight champion from Waterbury, fights Young McKenna at a smoker in the Top Notch Hall. Eddie Manning, baseball player, star amateur featherweight of Chelsea Mass, also boxes.

Beacon Falls gains a resident doctor. Dr. H.J. Blake of New York takes up his residence and sets up an office on Main Street. Dr. Blake is a graduate of the University of Indiana and besides having practiced for several years has had seven years' experience in the New York postgraduate Medical Hospital in New York. In 1916, long before the United States entered the World War, he went to France, joined the French Medical Corps and saw much service administrating aid to both the French and Italian troops on the Italian front. He is a native of Tennessee.

Reverend Cleveland Dierlam is the new minister of United Church; United Church enters fellowship of the Naugatuck Valley Association of Congressional churches.

Peter Rydzik is born December 12, and Michael Krenesky is born five hours later, December 13, on Railroad Avenue in the same apartment shared by two different parents, Mr. and Mr. Leo Rydzik and Mr. and Mrs. Stephen Krenesky.

1921 United States Rubber Company takes over the Beacon Falls Rubber Shoe Company, after the sudden death of Mr. Tracy Lewis, keeping the Beacon Falls plant as a subsidiary of the parent company and still maintaining the Top Notch trademark.

September 8: The White Eagle Society is organized and becomes known as the White Eagle Society Lodge No. 2128 of the Polish National Alliance.

Dr. David H. Bluestone moves to town to become the resident doctor. Dr. Bluestone had served in the U.S. Army for the past three years, having been stationed at the U.S. Army General Hospital No. 25 at Fort Benjamin Franklin near Indianapolis, Indiana. He is a graduate of the University of Syracuse. Dr. Bluestone has three years' experience in Mount Sinai lying-in hospital in New York City, the largest maternity hospital in the United States, and was with the Health Department in New York City, taking care of all contagious diseases and tuberculosis for one year. Dr. Bluestone is a specialist of the heart and lungs but is prepared to look after any illnesses that may occur in town and can be located at his new home, 40 Wolfe Avenue, or by telephone at 374-4.

The United States Rubber Company sells its building on Main Street to the Town of Beacon Falls for a town hall.

1922 Beacon Hose Company moves into new quarters, bottom of town hall on Main Street.

Kindergarten classes are established in the Beacon Falls school system. A two-story, four-room brick building is added to north side of original school (Center School). Cost: $16,244.81 (present town hall).

Polish residents (largest ethnic immigration group) form the White Eagle Society, affiliated with the St. Mary's Society and the Kosciusko Lodge No. 2128, founded in 1915.

Two changes occur during the school year. Miss Reynolds resigns to accept an appointment in her hometown, and Mrs. Madigan, who taught first grade and evening school, leaves on account of a death in her family. Two new teachers are added, and each teacher now has but one grade at the Center School.

Charles D. Roberts, health officer, reports that the schoolhouses in town are in good condition for the fall term, with some very much needed repairs having been done.

During the year, the town is very fortunate in not having any epidemics and diseases, having been reported very punctually.

Vital statistics: Population 1,800, Births 38, Deaths 10, Deaths under 5 years 9.

At the request of the state superintendent, the services of a visiting nurse is secured from the Red Cross Chapter in Naugatuck. The first school doctor is also hired. The Chicoskis start a grocery business on Main Street.

White Eagle Hall is built on Beacon Street

November 29: Meeting is held in Top Notch Hall to organize a free public library.

December 12: Election of officers is held in library. By-laws are read and accepted.

December 27: Special Town Meeting is held to give $200 to the Beacon Falls Library Association, as well as a room in Center School.

The new minister of United Church is Reverend Thomas Campbell.

942 people are employed at the Beacon Falls Rubber Shoe Company.

1923 January 31: Library is opened to the public.

August 30: Beacon Hose Company returns from West Haven parade with some loving cups. One prize was for most men in line: 37. It also won the tug of war. Cyrus Wilcox won the fifty-yard dash for men over fifty years of age. Herbert Borg won the one-hundred-yard dash.

Closing of old Nyumph School (Bethany Road), with Miss Lila Houghtaling as teacher.

1924 A new one-room Nyumph School is built on Feldspar Avenue (Pisani Home) and would be used until 1954. Miss Mable Chatfield, teacher, would teach four grades for thirty years.

A part-time music teacher is hired for Center School.

First Annual Ball of the Beacon Falls Top Notch Club is held at George's Hall in Seymour.

November 15: Reverend J.J. McAuliffe becomes first resident pastor of St. Michael's Church. He lived in one of the Homer D. Bronson Co. homes on Bethany Road.

The School District Speaking Contest is held at the Top Notch Hall, won by Miss Etta Esposito. In the state contest in Hartford, she would be awarded second place.

Center School makes arrangements with the Beacon Falls Rubber Shoe Company to use the Top Notch Theater for fundraisers to raise money to purchase new playground equipment at the school on College Avenue. Students raise $300 by selling tickets to the movies. When installed, exercises are held to celebrate the opening of the new playground at Center School.

Mr. Minor from Naugatuck visits the Center School regularly and gives instructions in music.

Naugatuck Chapter of the Red Cross extends services of Miss Shea, RN, one day a week.

1925 Pinesbridge Cemetery Association is formed. Beacon Falls turns the town cemetery over to the Pinesbridge Cemetery Association.

1927 Complete radio outfit is installed in Center School. All rooms are wired, loud speakers are placed in each room and the set itself, a Stromberg-Carlson, is placed in the eighth-grade room.

Fife-Drum Corps is organized at Center School.

1928 Reorganization of the evening school for foreign adults takes place under the direction of Miss Am Cullen. Twenty-nine men and six women register. Average attendance is fifteen. The town receives four dollars for each pupil from the state in average attendance.

The basement room of Center School is redecorated and fitted out with tables and benches to conduct a better organization for those who bring their lunches.

A music teacher, Mrs. Charles Manweiler, is added to the school system.

Beacon Falls Rubber Company gives use of its theater to Center School to run motion pictures, and the proceeds from this and the sale of candles by the school pupils enables them to purchase a new piano for the school.

Edna Fitzpatrick and Helen Meleski win honors in the spelling contest, conducted by the *Waterbury Republican*. Clara Killian would win the spelling contest held by the state in Hartford.

By special request, the Top Notch Theater runs three movies per week, providing attendance warrants it.

A Father and Son banquet is held at the United Church.

1929 Departmental system of instruction is introduced for seventh and eighth grades.

Beacon Hose Company purchases a new Seagrave fire truck.

The state buys the old Beacon Falls Rubber Co. Hotel on Main Street.

1930 Beacon Falls Rubber Shoe Company (United States Rubber Co.) president Clint Little announces that April 15, 1930, is the last day of making rubber shoe products in Beacon Falls. All manufacturing is moved to Naugatuck. Henceforth the buildings here would be used only for warehousing.

United States Rubber Co. changes its name to Uniroyal.

Reverend Henry Coleman is the new pastor at St. Michael's.

June 30: Daisy Rogers resigns as librarian. Maude A. Eggleton is appointed.

June 30: Beacon Hose Company No. 1 incorporates as of this date.

State Police open Station "I" under the command of Lieutenant Henry Albright; July 1: Command of Station "I" passes to William Schatzman.

At present, 25 percent of all valley resident are foreign born. Of the 49,382 people in Ansonia, Beacon Falls, Derby, Seymour and Shelton, 13,219 are foreign born.

1931 March 6: Parent Teachers Association in town is formed.

Town library acquires new shelves, additional magazines and books donated by interested residents.

1933 All classrooms in Center School are self-contained, and the same teacher instructs all subjects.

Beacon Falls Rubber Shoe Company name on the two towers is replaced by the name Uniroyal.

William Dubay of Beacon Falls wins the New England wood chopping championship at the Eastern States Exposition in West Springfield, Massachusetts, by chopping down a ten-inch-diameter tree and cutting it into three lengths in two minutes, fourteen seconds.

1934 April 21: Supper to raise funds is held at United Church Hall. The delicious meal is thirty-five cents for adults, twenty cents for those under twelve.

May: Present rectory of St. Michael's Church on Maple Avenue is occupied. Rectory previously was a rented home on Bethany Road (Homer D. Bronson Co. home).

February 20: Eleven inches of snow and a thirty-five-mile wind paralyze the area.

1935 Dance is held at Henry Smith Dance Hall netting $127 for the library. Eighteen organizations contributed $1 each for expenses.

Reverend H. Cyrus Higgins succeeds Reverend Coleman, who was transferred to Bridgeport, at St. Michael's Church.

October 26: The Wooden Bridge, built in 1856, is replaced by a most modern, up-to-date steel structure. Gammino Construction Co. of Providence, Rhode Island, was contractor. 212 feet in length and 45 feet width, with walks on both side for pedestrians.

Reverend Craig Whitsett is the new minister of United Church.

1936 Sheriff Peter Kaminski of town is killed in Milford.

1937 May: Freak storm hits Beacon Falls. Damage estimated in the thousands; hundreds of windows shattered. Warner House on Lopus Road loses roof, and Post Home on Bethany Road loses its porch. Smith Farm silo is also knocked down.

June 20: Trolley service is discontinued. Mr. Bontempo pulls switch at the power station at midnight as last southbound trolley passes through town.

Bus service is started to replace trolley by Connecticut Light and Power Company.

Reverend Ellis Veale takes over at United Church.

1938 Reverend Jerome Cook succeeds Reverend Higgins at St. Michael's Church.

Hurricane hits Connecticut.

December: Beacon Falls Recreation Club is organized.

1939 Miss Susan Cocchiola is appointed the school nurse and health teacher. Prior to this, Loretta Shea, Mary Claffey and Catherine Brooks—school nurses since 1922—were under the supervision of the Naugatuck Red Cross.

1940 Post No. 25, American Legion, reactivates as Schaeffer-Fischer Post (name derived from Fred Schaeffer from World War I and William Fischer of World War II).

1941 April 8: American Legion Auxiliary Unit No. 25 is formed.

June: Building of new St. Michael's Church on Maple Avenue is begun.

July 31: Old wooden church on Main Street is sold to State Highway Commission for $16,500.

August: State Police leaves Beacon Falls, opens new Station "I" in Bethany.

September 20: State returns old church building to church, and church sells building separately. Wood from building is dismantled and used to build a house in Naugatuck.

September 21: Cornerstone laid in 1899 is removed by Father Cook following the final Mass.

September 22: Weekday Masses are held at rectory on Maple Avenue, and Sunday Masses are held at Top Notch Movie House on Main Street.

Officers of American Legion Auxiliary Unit No. 25:
President: Mrs. Harriet Evans
Vice President: Mrs. Irene Rung
Treasure: Mrs. Edith Witherwax
Historian: Mrs. Helen Donlan
Chaplain: Mrs. Christine Classey
Sgt. at Arms: Mrs. Florence Wynne

Reverend Millard Stevens is new minister of United Church.

October: Cornerstone of new St. Michael's Church is laid during impressive ceremonies by the Most Reverend Maurice F. McAuliffe, bishop of Hartford.

December 7: Empire of Japan bombs Pearl Harbor. Start of World War II for the United States.

1942 February: 120 men in Beacon Falls between the ages of twenty and forty-five sign up for draft registration.

June 26: Mass is celebrated in new St. Michael's, although the interior is not completed.

1943 Ceremonies are held for the unveiling of the Honor Roll on Main Street.

Reverend Harry Thomas is the new minister of United Church.

1944 Pupils of the Center School take part in the raising their new Minute Man flag for attaining 90 percent goal in the sale of defense stamps.

1945 April 4: Mary Ann Rung is the first delegate to Girls State American Legion, sponsored by Post No. 25 Auxiliary.

V-E Day.

Public dance is held at the Beacon Falls Recreation Hall, sponsored by the Beacon Falls Veterans Memorial Fund Committee.

V-J Day, World War II is over.

1946 Rimmon School closes. Miss Valentine Mikulich is the last teacher.

Street lighting increased to forty-seven lampposts.

Welcome Home Parade is held for World War II veterans; more than 250 men and women answered the call.

October: Democratic administration is elected to office, with Frank Semplenski (D) elected First Selectman.

Reverend Donald E. Bartlett is new minister of United Church.

1947 March 28: Many homes and businesses are razed by State Highway Commission. The Board of Selectmen, with the help of state representatives, is asked to put a stop to this action.

1948 Mr. Albert Eggleton is appointed town librarian at thirty-five dollars per month, replacing Miss Maude Eggleton.

Hot lunches are instituted at Center School.

American Legion takes over home on Main Street (old Church House) from the Homer D. Bronson Co.

State aid for roads is changed by the state legislature. Beacon Falls is cut from $43,000 per year to $20,000.

August 6: Town Meeting votes to install sewer trunk line from Church Street to Bethany Road. This was incorporated in bid by the State of Connecticut in conjunction with construction of Route 8. Cost approximately $32,000, saving the town between $10,000 and $15,000.

New town vault is built at Center School in anticipation of the school becoming the new town hall.

October: Stoddard Place is accepted as town road by the town.

Beacon Hose Company and American Legion sponsor Halloween party and parade for children of town.

Reverend S. Alexander Harper is the next minister of United Church.

1949 April: Sewer trunk line is built.

Town of Beacon Falls adopts biennial elections.

October: Gruber Road is accepted.

Option is taken on two sites for a new school.

Committee is formed of members of the American Legion, veterans and the Board of Selectmen to study advisability of renaming some streets after deceased veterans.

1950 August: Community ambulance service begins with the donation of a Packard hearse by the Buckmiller family.

May: Town purchases a portion of the Clark property that borders Highland Avenue for a new school.

June: Board of Selectmen appoints Sewer Authority.

October: Building permit ordinance is adopted.

Androsko Road is accepted.

Reverend Donald E. Bartlett returns to preach at United Church.

Revaluation of all property in the town of Beacon Falls takes place.

Harold Benz is elected fire chief, succeeding William ("Pop") Lee, who had served as chief since 1907. Pop Lee, an original charter member, still maintains his membership in the fire company.

1951 Local school board informs members of library association that it desires the library room for schoolroom purposes. Library association votes to contact the First Selectman to see if the board would consider moving the Rimmon Schoolhouse adjacent to the town hall to use as a library.

March: Town stops further gravel excavation in gravel bank on Church Street.

May: Issuance of bonds for installation of sewers on Burton Road; Fairfield Place; Avenues A, B, C and D; Feldspar Avenue; and Bethany Road is authorized.

June: Revaluation is completed. A fair and equalized system is inaugurated for assessments on all properties.

July: Ordinance is created for sewer inspector and public health authority.

George Rau is elected fire chief after the sudden death of Harold Benz.

1952 January: It is decided that if no suitable place can be found for a library, the library will remain in the town hall.

Library association is disbanded at the end of the school year.

February: School Survey Committee is appointed.

Town purchases three voting machines.

August: Town extends rent control after this was curtailed at the state level.

Town approves participation of town employees in Social Security.

Mrs. Catherine Rupsis is appointed school nurse and health teacher.

1953 January: Application is made for a state grant for new school construction—a proposed fourteen-room school for 420 pupils.

Miss Evelyn Hassan is appointed Special Policewoman, first woman police officer in town history.

January 20: School Building Committee is appointed: Walter A. Muroff, chairman; Albert Kievman, secretary; William Loftus; Frank Semplenski; Frank Bronson; Edward Smith; Kenneth Upright; George Lafferty; George Leeper; J. Arthur Hackett; and Joseph Hagen.

April: American Legion Auxiliary Unit No. 25 is officially accepted.

Ordinance creating Zoning and Planning Commission passes.

June: Town library closes. Books are packed and stored at Rimmon Schoolhouse.

September: Bond issue of $387,000 for construction of new school is authorized.

Report of Recreation Committee (Edward Bea, chairman): ice rink is made but fails due to weather; site for new ball field is considered (Gruber Field, off Lopus Road); and town swimming pool is proposed because of lack of parking at Bronson Pond.

October: Nine hundred feet of railroad track are removed and replaced at High Rock Glen after broken wheel causes pileup of a sixty-two-car freight train; twelve cars derailed. $75.000 damage.

Beacon Falls Lions Club holds Charter Night dinner and dance at Sullivan's Inn in Cotton Hollow.

1954 March: Town purchases new fire truck for $21,500.

Reverend John J. Sobolewski is the new pastor at St. Michael's Church.

Beacon Hose and Community Club donates $1,000 each and purchases new ambulance from Naugatuck. Old ambulance is sold to Oxford to start its ambulance service.

November: New campus-type school is put into service.

December: Formal dedication of Laurel Ledge School; name suggested by Mrs. Loretta Baukat.

Nyumph School is closed; all classes are to attend the new Laurel.

Ledge School. Miss Mable Chatfield, who has taught at Nyumph since 1924, also moves to the new school.

Zoning ordinance repealed and replaced by stop-gap ordinance.

Formation of the first active Children of Mary Sodality under the supervision of Reverend John J. Sobolewski.

Reverend Andrew Solandt takes over as new minister of United Church.

1955 June: Stoddard Road Extension is accepted by the town. Shasta Terrace is also accepted.

August: Raffles Law referendum is recommended to be put on voting machines at next election.

BLACK FRIDAY FLOODS, results of Hurricanes Connie and Diane. Town of Beacon Falls borrows $15,000 for flood relief.

October: Temporary Planning Commission is created to deal with aftermath of the flooding, with Chairman Ernest Trzaski and members Patsy Mennillo, Leon Mendlesohn, Ralph Tucker and Michael Krenesky. Redevelopment Commission is also created; both commissions will work with state-supplied planning consultants Gates and Ford, Salem Shapiro Associates.

Beacon Falls suffers $2.3 million in property losses due to the flood.

1956 March: After the Flood of '55, Redevelopment Agency is authorized to make application to federal government for financial assistance of two-thirds of the cost of an urban renewal project, on a preliminary survey in the Pinesbridge area.

Committee is created to allocate numbers to homes for mail delivery service by foot carrier.

May: Town releases old town hall building on Main Street to the Beacon Hose Co. to be used as firehouse.

Brick portion of Center School becomes the new town hall.

Recommended razing of wooden portion of Center School and replacing it for use as the town garage.

Town accepts Summerfield and Trackson Streets in Beacon Manor section of town.

Highland Street Extension, Buckingham Road and Edgewood Drive are accepted as town roads.

June 10: Mass is celebrated in completed edifice of St. Michael's Church.

June 24: Dedication of new St. Michael's Church takes place.

October: Town repays flood loan of $15,000.

Mercury lighting system is installed on Route 8 from Church Street to South Main Street for pedestrian and motor vehicle safety.

Street lighting is increased from 47 to 121. State engineers install pedestrian crosswalks, safety signs and traffic regulation signs on Route 8 (Main Street).

Arthur Smith is elected chief of Beacon Hose Company.

1957 American Legion Post No. 25, with State 40 & 8, donates first wheelchair for town use.

New post office is dedicated on Main Street, with John J. Lee, postmaster.

New fire phone service is installed for Beacon Hose Company.

Town votes to reopen library. $2,000 is appropriated. Mrs. Martin Christensen is appointed librarian, with Mrs. Victor Zollo and Mrs. David Thompson as assistants.

Plans are set up for new addition to Laurel Ledge School.

Eighth-grade students under the direction of Miss Carruba and Mr. Dierenzo take a bus trip to New York to witness performance of Ringling Bros. Circus at Madison Square Garden.

Eighth-grade class concludes study of Connecticut and its government by taking a trip to Hartford and the General Assembly, where they are introduced to the House of Representatives by Mrs. Clara O'Shea, our state representative.

1958 Veterans Monument is erected and dedicated on the front lawn of town hall in memory of deceased veterans of all wars.

Democratic Women's Club of Beacon Falls is established, with State Representative Clara O'Shea as first president.

Thomas Fitzpatrick Memorial Award is established, given to student graduating from Laurel Ledge School for highest mark in social studies.

Departmental system for grades seven and eight is created at Laurel Ledge School.

Mrs. Margaret B. Donahue retires after thirty and a half years in the Beacon Falls School System. She is replaced by Mr. Russell Smith as principal.

State fire marshal gives the town twenty-four hours to stop using one room in the town hall building for a classroom. Reshuffling of pupils and use of a small library room in the administration building remedies the problem for the remainder of the year.

A fifth building completes the campus of Laurel Ledge School. This will house the seventh and eighth grades and will be organized on a modified junior high school plan.

1959 Beacon Falls Cub Scout Pack 100, a part of the Southeast District of Waterbury Council, is organized. Mr. Louis Cretella is the first cubmaster.

Reverend Herbert J. Clarkin is appointed first assistant pastor at St. Michael's Church.

April: Library is finally opened, with three thousand volumes donated by local residents.

An educational program for mentally disabled children is organized under the direction of Mr. Harold Ogle.

Reverend R.A. Clarke is the new minister of United Church.

Nursery class is started at United Church under the direction of Mrs. Ethel Sullivan and Mrs. Vivien Smith.

Miss Mable Chatfield retires after thirty-five years in the Beacon Falls School System. Laurel Ledge has a teaching staff of seventeen teachers, the largest ever in the history of the town.

Beacon Falls files application for moneys under the new National Defense Education Act of 1958. This act is the first breakthrough for educating in twenty-five to thirty years.

1960 An additional exit to St. Michael's Church Lyceum is constructed to meet the stringent state fire laws.

Formation of a Ladies Auxiliary of Beacon Hose Company.

January: Construction of a community recreation area off Pent Road is in full swing. The project is under the direction of the Town Recreation Commission, with the cooperation of the Beacon Falls Lions Club. Mr. John J. Lee, chairman of the commission, and Mr. George Bronson are assisting in area layout.

June: Michael Krenesky is elected president of the United Steelworkers of America, Local 5104, Homer D. Bronson Company.

Due to a growing school population, additional classroom space must be provided. Seventy pupils are expected in grade one. Three teachers are needed, but only two can be hired because there are only two classrooms available.

1961 The Beacon Falls Republican Club is organized with the encouragement of Mrs. Harry Cooper and the help of state officials.

The library acquires a reading room and additional shelves to accommodate growing adult nonfiction collection. Hours are increased to thirteen hours per week.

May: Daniel Lee Jr. is the new chief of Beacon Hose Company.

State trooper Michael Muggieo is assigned from Litchfield barracks as resident trooper.

Constable Howard Enquist is seriously injured in a hit-and-run accident.

Mrs. Connie Belanger is appointed policewoman.

Beacon Falls Jaycees holds second annual Children's Film Festival at Laurel Ledge School auditorium.

The boys' baseball team of Laurel Ledge wins league championship. Beacon Falls Lions Club presents the team with a league trophy.

1962 Bus service by Connecticut Light and Power is discontinued.

Intercity Company starts hourly bus service between Waterbury and Bridgeport.

Two hundred production workers strike at Homer D. Bronson Company.

Reverend R. Ward is the new minister at United Church.

July: Mr. Russell Smith resigns as principal of Laurel Ledge, to be replaced by Mrs. Frances Russell, who had taught seventh and eighth grades at the school.

1963 Mrs. David Thompson resigns as assistant librarian and is replaced by Mrs. Bernard Drabicki.

Mrs. Helene Colburn is appointed school secretary at Laurel Ledge.

Plans are made for another addition to Laurel Ledge School.

Until his death this year, charter member William "Pop" Lee was an active member of Beacon Hose Company.

The Board of Education raises teacher salaries by $200 on the minimum and $100 on the maximum. This makes the bachelor column $4,600 to $7,300 and the masters $4,900 to $7,600, both in twelve steps.

Sports program is organized under the direction of Mr. Kruger, Mr. Fitzmaurice, Mr. Hutter and Miss Forst at Laurel Ledge School.

1964 New educational wing is constructed at United Church.

Mr. Ward Wilson is ordained in United Church.

Reverend Clarkin transferred and replaced by Reverend Jon S. Ahern.

Mr. Harold W. Wilcox retires after fifty years as clerk for J.J. O'Connell and owner of H.W. Wilcox store on Main Street in Beacon Falls. J.J. O'Connell took over the store in 1912, and Mr. Wilcox went to work for him in 1914.

Michael Krenesky and his wife, Beverly, take over the H.W. Wilcox Patent Medicines store from Mr. Harold W. Wilcox.

Mentally handicapped program is discontinued, and children are transferred to schools in other towns that are better equipped to handle these issues.

Educational trips are made to Peabody Museum, Bridgeport Museum of Arts and Science, Stamford Museum, Chipaug Dam and the World's Fair by Laurel Ledge students.

New six-room school building to house seventh and eighth grades is completed at Laurel Ledge Elementary School.

1965 Kindergarten classes are held in St. Michael's Church Lyceum.

A tax rate of 40 mills is laid on the list of October 1964, payable July 1 and January 1.

1966 Roger Brennan is elected chief of Beacon Hose Company.

Beacon Falls Board of Education is faced with more problems. The town of Seymour, Connecticut, has a housing problem and cannot take more Beacon Falls students.

Beacon Falls residents turn down formation of a Temporary Regional School Study with Prospect and Middlebury.

A magazine section is set up in the reading room of the town library.

1967 Formation of Beacon Falls Recreation League. This is the beginning of what later became the Beacon Falls Baseball League in 1968. The "vision" of a youth baseball league was started by Albert Borgnis. It led to the town acquiring the property that is now the Pent Road Recreation Complex.

September: New high-level span is built over river in Pinesbridge, named and dedicated as the Hearne W. Beaver Memorial Bridge. This is the first memorial in the state of Connecticut for a soldier killed in Vietnam.

Dental clinic is held at Laurel Ledge School, giving 246 youngsters cleaning and fluoride treatment.

642 children receive oral polio vaccine.

First aid is taught to the eighth-grade class and accepted as a helpful service.

1968 First year of operation of a new baseball league proves to be successful. With the advice and assistance of attorney Ronald Sarasin, the league is incorporated.

Gordon Vought is ordained as minister at United Church.

February: Beacon Falls Junior Woman's Club is established, sponsored by the Naugatuck Junior Woman's Club. First slate of officers:

President: Mrs. S. John Washburn
Vice President: Mrs. Ronald A. Sarasin
Rec. Secretary: Mrs. Richard Raymond III
Corres. Secretary: Mrs. George Lafferty Jr.
Treasurer: Mrs. Walter Carlson

Trooper Robert Malesky succeeds Michael Muggeo as resident trooper.

Town of Beacon Falls trades Main Street Building (firehouse) to the Beacon Falls Community Recreation Club Inc. for its land on Main Street for future building of a new firehouse.

Kindergarten classes are conducted in St. Michael's Church due to lack of space due to increased enrollment. Four separate classes are held daily.

Veterans Day (November 11) is shifted to the fourth Monday in October to increase the number of three-day holiday weekends.

Beacon Falls–Prospect Temporary Regional School Study Committee is established by vote at a Town Meeting. Beacon Falls members include:

Ernest Trzaski, Chairman
Marjorie Sarasin
Frank Semplenski
Reverend Eugene McAllister
Reverend John S. Ahearn
Edward Betkoski

1969 June: Beacon Falls Activity Club is organized. The main purpose is to influence the younger generation toward a constructive adolescence with the responsibility of community involvement and recreation.

Beacon Falls and Prospect vote to form Regional School District No. 16 by a vote total of 1,212 Yes, 300 No.

This has been a hazardous year. Two motor vehicle operators and one pedestrian have died and three pedestrians have been seriously injured after being struck by cars as they either walked along or crossed Route 8.

Police continue drive on speeders with a radar unit on Main Street.

Constables Walter Olsen, Gabriel Fuoco, Michael Dragalin and Martin Rau are operating the radar unit.

Pack 100 Cub Scouts hold Annual Frog and Turtle races.

Mrs. Frances Russell, former teacher and lately supervising principal, retires after forty-two years of service. Her final statement as principal is as follows: "An educational program within any community, will be no better than what the people of the community want it to be."

1970 Reverend Ahearn is transferred and replaced by Reverend Roger E. Laterreur.

June 30: Mrs. Helen Hurley retires as *Naugatuck News* correspondent covering Beacon Falls.

Mrs. Helene Colburn is named "Woman of the Year" by the Beacon Falls Junior Woman's Club.

Wastewater Treatment Plant is completed at total cost of $1.5 million. Net cost to town is $235,000.

1971: The Centennial Year

1971 January: Post office issues special cancellation commemorating the 100th anniversary of the town of Beacon Falls.

May 4: House Bill no. 774, an act concerning renaming High Rock State Park in Beacon Falls and Naugatuck the "Clara O'Shea Memorial State Park," in consideration of her great interest in and work on behalf of the park during her service in the General Assembly.

Lee Lennon is elected chief of Beacon Hose Company.

June 30: Beacon Falls celebrates the 100th anniversary of the incorporation of the town with a gala ten-day birthday party on the Laurel Ledge School grounds.

Special First Day Cover issued by the Centennial Committee. Requests for the cover came from all parts of the United States.

United Church celebrates its 100th anniversary on Wolfe Avenue.

Dedication of historical marker is held on the town hall lawn. Mr. Raymond Baldwin, ex-governor and ex-senator, is the honored guest for the dedication.

Sells and Gray Circus performs two shows at Gruber Field during Centennial Week.

138 members are enrolled in the "Brothers of the Brush" Society, reported by Chairman Kevin Swan.

Beacon Falls Community Development Action Plan (CDAP) is reorganized.

Robert Cole, advisor to the Beacon Falls Activity Club, is authorized to represent Beacon Falls at a Narco convention in New Haven to renew new drug rehabilitation methods.

Cub Pack 100, sponsored by Laurel Ledge PTA, holds Pinewood Derby.

Mrs. Ruth Cheskey is named "Woman of the Year" by the Beacon Falls Junior Woman's Club.

More than 650 persons attend the 71st Annual Ball of the Beacon Hose Company at Warsaw Park. Many of the ladies in attendance wear old-fashioned gowns in keeping with the Centennial year.

Hearing is held in Hartford concerning the "Nightmare Alley" portion of highway between Naugatuck and Beacon Falls. Also known as the "upper and lower road," too many fatalities and accidents in the past year have taken place.

Eighteen-year-olds are given the right to vote.

Dedication of Long River School in Prospect is held.

1972 Town of Beacon Falls purchases 325-acre Matthies property in Pinesbridge for $150,000.

First meeting of the Beacon Falls Board of Park Commission is held. The first order of business is for all members to meet for a walk in the new Matthies Park.

Fortieth anniversary of Reverend John J. Sobolewski, pastor of St. Michael's.

Town clerk and tax collector open new offices on the ground floor of town hall.

State installs traffic light at intersection of Route 42 East and Route 8, meant to alleviate entrance and exit traffic from the Homer D. Bronson Company.

Cub Scout Pack 116 cleans up lower area of High Rock Park, in keeping with the monthly theme "Keep America Beautiful."

On behalf of the Town of Beacon Falls, First Selectman James Greene offers forty acres of Matthies Park property to Region No. 16 Board of Education for use as a high school site for a price of $40,000.

Newspaper editorial comments on Regional High School Building Committee executive session on high school site selections.

1973 January 10: Resident Trooper William Dudley is presented with keys to a new police cruiser, the first in the history of the town, by First Selectman James Greene at ceremonies at town hall.

Beacon Falls Seniors organizes as a club.

Ansonia Savings Bank comes to town on Main Street.

Congressman Ronald Sarasin provides American flag (flown over U.S. Capitol) to the Beacon Hose Company.

Waste Water Treatment Plant is built on Lopez Road.

Beacon Falls Ridge Runners holds horse show at the Recreation Field.

1974 Prospect sues the Town of Beacon Falls over equalization of assets. Its claim is for $122,000, whereas the town claims only $60,000. The town has already paid $24,000.

Merchants and businessmen contribute moneys to Beacon Falls Baseball League for the purchase of bleachers for the Little League field on Pent Road.

Beacon Falls Ridge Runners hold open horse show at the Pent Road field.

Beacon Falls Hose Company holds Diamond Jubilee Dinner Dance at Preston Hill Inn in Middlebury, Connecticut.

A new Case bucket loader is purchased by the town.

1975 Beacon Falls Bicentennial Committee is formed under the authorization of the Board of Selectmen. Jack Betkoski is appointed as chairman by the board, with other elected officers including Vice Chairman Fred George, Treasurer Mildred Jurzynski and Secretary Karen Wilson.

Brown University Hall of Fame inducts William Karaban (excelled in football).

Five-member Housing Authority is created at a Town Meeting. Robert Tiano is named chairman by the Board of Selectmen. Other officers include Vice Chairman David Conroy, Secretary James Capasso, Treasurer Charles Debarber and Assistant Treasurer Domenic Daunis.

Night lights are installed for ice skating at Matthies Pond.

Beacon Hose Company holds a regional simulated disaster exercise with other fire companies at the Beacon Falls–Bethany Town Line on Route 42.

Laurel Garden Club is organized in Beacon Falls.

Beacon Falls builds a new town garage on Lopus Road.

Unpaid taxes concern Beacon Falls officials. The Board of Selectmen votes to release list to press for publication.

Riot-equipped state troopers from all parts of the state are called to High Rock Park to calm down the Annual Good Friday event held by college and high school students.

United Steelworkers Local No. 5104 strikes at the Homer D. Bronson Company.

Beacon Falls rejects Housing Authority report on feasibility of constructing elderly housing in town.

Beacon Falls Bicentennial Commission presents "Spirit of '76" family picnic at Pent Road Recreation Field. This is the official Beacon Falls Bicentennial "kick-off."

The Beacon Falls Tea Party is held aboard the *M/V Martha's Vineyard* by the Bicentennial Festivals Committee.

Board of Park Commissioners sets up rules and regulations for boating on Matthies, following Connecticut General Statutes 15-136.

July 7: Planning and Zoning Commission moves public hearing on Greyhound racetrack outdoors when four hundred people show up to hear the facts.

August 8: Sixty people are in attendance at a general review held on application submitted to the State Gaming Commission.

Taxpayers For the Track organizational meeting is held. The following officers are elected:

Co-Chairman: James Greene and John Betkoski
Secretary: Michael Krenesky
Treasurer: Thomas Halloway

Citizens Against the Track (CATT) is formed by seventeen residents, in opposition to the $10 million racetrack proposed by Harney Associates Ltd. Officers elected include:

President: Mrs. Kathy Shugdinis
Vice President: Raymond Wilson
Secretary: Mrs. Ethel Reigel
Treasurer: Mrs. Carol Zinko

Formal Bicentennial flag raising ceremonies are held at Laurel Ledge School; a color guard is provided by U.S. Marine Corps Reserve, 4th Marine Division.

November 4: Region No. 16 teachers strike, picket four Region schools.

President Ford signs legislation restoring observation of Veterans Day to original date of November 11, to take effect in 1978.

1976 March: The U.S. Supreme Court rules that "one man, one vote" concept be applied to regional school boards. This decision upholds the ruling made in 1972. Going forward, weighted voting based on student population would set future discontent in Beacon Falls with the Regional School System.

Beacon Hose Company Yankees defeat White Eagle Society Eagles, 16–4, and the Schaeffer-Fischer Post Tigers win, 17–0, over the P&R Construction Dodgers to open the 1976 Beacon Falls Baseball League season.

May: Beacon Falls Ridge Runners holds an open horse show.

Laurel Garden Club becomes member of the Federated Garden Club of Connecticut.

Frank DelVecchio succeeds Lee Lennon as chief of Beacon Hose Company.

July: Beacon Falls Bicentennial Committee starts weekend activities with an informal dance at Pennyroyal Lodge in Seymour.

The Horizons '76 dedication of the Bernard H. Matthies Memorial Park is held. Planning of the program was done by Mrs. Beverly Krenesky, chairman of Horizons '76, and Mr. Jack Betkoski, chairman of the bicentennial committee. Mr. James Greene is master of ceremonies; Selectmen Leonard D'Amico and John Betkoski and First Selectman Garry Fuoco also take part.

Bicentennial dedication of the new bandstand is held at Matthies Park, a replica of the bandstand that once stood on the Town Green on Main Street. This is to be a lasting memorial in observance of the bicentennial of these United States. A Festivals Committee, with John Massaua as chairman, assists in the occasion.

Car sticker system goes into effect for identification at town parks.

October: President Harold Murtha of the Valley Greyhound Park requests for a referendum for a public opinion poll indicating whether or not residents favor a dog track.

One thousand residents attend picnic and greased pig event held at Pent Road Recreation Park on Memorial Day at the "Spirit of '76" picnic.

Beacon Falls votes to withdraw from the Regional School District No. 16 due to the "one man, one vote" Supreme Court decision.

1977 Region No. 16 parents, some marching with preschool children, picket Algonquin School.

AutoSwage Products purchases twenty-thousand-square-foot building off Church Street.

Referendum is held for opinion poll on a dog track. DEFEATED.

August: Beacon Falls Jaycees present "Saturday Night in the Park," a summer night musical experience at beautiful Matthies Park.

1978 Veterans Day returns to November 11.

1979 Laurel Ledge PTA holds first annual Fun Fair.

Inaugural issue of the *Town Crier* newsletter is published.

State closes Murtha Dump on Blackberry Hill.

Beacon Hose Company Fantasy Day is held at Matthies Park.

Community Health Service is established in Beacon Falls.

Establishment of an Economic Development Commission.

Beacon Falls Public Library holds 11,215 volumes; a total of 9,786 books circulated the year before, with a registration of 1,473 borrowers.

1980 Eleven-year-old school district shared by Beacon Falls and Prospect is in the midst of its fourth dissolution attempt by the Town of Beacon Falls.

April 26: First issue of the *Beacon Buzz* is published, a newspaper of the Beacon Falls Youth Club.

Uniroyal Warehouse building closes its doors—the end of an era that began with the Coe Tannery, circa 1840s, Home Woolen Company 1860s and the Beacon Falls Rubber Shoe Company, 1899.

New streetlights are to be upgraded as steps to improve pedestrian safety.

Mudslide on Route 8 forces shutdown of northbound lane near Route 42 in Pinesbridge.

December 7: Rededication of the Sanctuary of St. Michael's Church.

1981 Revaluation of all properties in the town of Beacon Falls.

Rimmon Hill Road is accepted as a town road.

Residents Against Polluting the Environment (RAPE) formed in opposition to a proposed PCB warehouse. Residents march in protest of the proposed warehouse.

Toll-free calling in the Naugatuck exchange begins.

May: Harold Lennon is elected new fire chief of Beacon Hose Company.

The Beacon Falls Community Recreation Club disbands and returns the building to the Town of Beacon Falls, according to deed of 1968.

December 19: More than two hundred people attend ribbon-cutting ceremonies at the new Senior Center on Main Street.

1983 November 13: Three hundred children are fingerprinted at Laurel Ledge School in a PTO-sponsored event.

1984 Beacon Falls Park and Recreation Commission holds its annual fishing derby at Matthies Park; 118 youths sixteen and under participate.

Troop 104 Boy Scouts of America is reorganized, with Beacon Hose Company as sponsor and Long River Council commissioner Andrew Rozum, Ned Grace and Milton DeGeorge as committeemen.

Dedication of the American Flag Memorial for all Vietnam veterans in memory of Captain Joseph P. Holland of Naugatuck, a good friend of Harold Murtha, is held at the Murtha Industrial Park off Railroad Avenue.

A 1,750-foot public water line is installed up Blackberry Hill.

A Suicide Awareness Valuable Education (SAVE) program to educate the community to help prevent teenage suicides is started under the leadership of Lieutenant Robert Cole of the Beacon Hose Company.

Former First Selectman Mario Fuoco dies unexpectedly, stunning the town.

Planning and Zoning Commission considers changing zoning regulations to allow Uniroyal Complex to be converted to condominiums and offices.

1985 Tragic fire on Main Street claims the lives of two young people.

June: Beacon Hose Company rushes food to tornado victims in Beaver Falls, Pennsylvania.

A section of modernized Route 8 that passes through the Naugatuck State Forest area receives "Excellence in Highway Design" award.

The Store House at the Beacon Mill Village opens.

The Town of Beacon Falls purchases forty-two wooded acres off Frontage Road, "The Road to Nowhere," from the State Department of Transportation, protecting the town's woodland from any future exploitation. Residents, in an 85-10 vote, agree to purchase for $83,000 the two parcels.

EPA Superfund decides to clean up Beacon Heights Landfill on Blackberry Hill Road.

After sixteen years, issue of equalization of assets with Prospect is finally settled. Beacon Falls owes Prospect $38,000, as $24,000 had previously been paid. Prospect was originally looking for $122,000.

1986 May: Joseph Daddona is elected fire chief, succeeding Harold Lennon.

The Connecticut State Firemen's Association votes Harold Lennon as 1985's Outstanding Firefighter for efforts to have every house in town equipped with a smoke detector.

1987 Selectmen appoint Mr. Conrad Dahm, Town Park and Recreation employee, to patrol Matthies Park and Recreation Field to combat vandalism.

1988 April 26: Two-question referendum is up for voters of Beacon Falls: "#1. Shall the Town of Beacon Falls withdraw from Regional District #16?" Town residents vote no. "#2. Shall the Town of Beacon Falls participate in the construction of a High School for Regional District #16?" Town residents vote yes. This was just the opposite of the referendum held on September 2, 1976, when the voters voted 621-83 to leave the district.

Pent Road Recreation area snack bar is broken into, with fifty cases of coke, thirty boxes of candy, all hot-dogs and hamburgers and a microwave oven stolen.

June 8: Town is faced with another high school referendum, which is rejected by more than nine hundred votes.

About seventy-five people attend the rededication of the eighty-eight-year-old church bell on St. Michael's Church lawn in memory of Chester Trzaski. The bell originally was located at the old church on Main Street.

Reverend John J. Stronkowski, newly ordained to the priesthood, celebrates his first Mass at St. Michael's Church.

Father Ahern holds annual Halloween Mass.

Miss Adrienne LaMorte is appointed as the town's second full-time resident state trooper.

Town of Beacon Falls creates a sidewalk ordinance.

Michael Krenesky is appointed official town historian, a newly created position.

1989 March: Great Country Bank is robbed.

Neighborhood Watch program on Rimmon Hill area forms to assist Trooper Paul Heon.

Town of Beacon Falls passes town ordinance on removal of ice and snow from all sidewalks.

June 13: Region votes for $5 million expansion for Laurel Ledge School.

Reverend Leonard Kvedas succeeds Father Ahern at St. Michael's Church.

Mandated by the State of Connecticut, the Town of Beacon Falls forms a Historical Commission. Officers include Chairman John Packer; Vice Chairman Leonard Greene; Secretary Clementine Cardow; and Dorothy Mayer, Agnes Packer and non-voting member Town Historian Michael Krenesky.

A referendum for a $1.2 million renovation and improvements to Pent Road passes.

1990 The Connecticut Historical Commission identifies twenty-five buildings in Beacon Falls that might be classified as "historic." A $1,750 grant was administrated by the State Department of Housing for this study.

Beacon Falls Lions Club ships more than twelve thousand audio tapes collected by Bill Franks of Naugatuck to Westover Air Force Base for shipment to the troops in Saudi Arabia.

1991 The Connecticut Stands Together Rally to support the troops in the Persian Gulf is held at the firehouse.

James Greene, former First Selectman, and Fire Chief Robert Cole both die. The town loses two great men.

Beacon Falls Hawks win soccer championship.

Ceremonies are held at the opening of the baseball field behind the Laurel Ledge School, due to renovations at the Pent Road facility.

1992 Dedication of the new Beacon Falls Recreation Complex on Pent Road is held.

New elevator is installed in the town hall.

Fishermen are happy to hear that salmon are being stocked in the Naugatuck River.

The town mourns death of Fire Marshal Harold Lennon. Son Sean Lennon is appointed fire marshal to follow in the steps of his father.

1993 Renovations in the town hall give the First Selectman an office of his own.

Cleanup of Beacon Heights begins. Parents ask for fence at the toxic landfill.

Beacon Falls Lions build a gazebo on the grounds at St. Michael's Church as a gift to the community.

The Beacon Falls Public Library plans to upgrade services.

The Beacon Falls Historical Society dates one of the early houses in town with a plaque: the Sheldon Clark House on the Clark Farm off Clark Lane, circa 1835.

1994 January 5: Beacon Falls Town Clerk Francis X. Doiron calls it a career after forty-seven years on the job—a job well done.

A Christian Concert in the Park featuring Ms. Tina Wills is presented at St. Michael's.

First edition of *Naugy Talk News* is published, including Beacon Falls "Peekin at Beacon."

1995 January: Members of the Beacon Hose Company No. 1 ask Selectmen to create a fund to financially reward firefighters and ambulance personnel over the age of sixty-seven.

Town officials plan for the 125th birthday celebration of the town of Beacon Falls. Clem and Bill Cardow, cochairmen; Jack Betkoski; Mike Krenesky; and Thomas and Diane Laput make up committee. More members to follow.

Former Town Clerk Francis X. Doiron dies after a brief illness.

Beacon Falls makes plans to host twenty-six Slovenian Special Olympians and their coaches.

Citizens for Change, the town's third party, announces nine candidates named for the fall municipal election.

The Beacon Falls Historical Society presents "Archaeology of the Naugatuck Valley." Dr. Nicholas Bellatoni, state archaeologist, is guest speaker.

Laurel Ledge School offers one-stop shopping for schoolchildren by opening a store in the school cafeteria.

April 25: Long River $8.6 million Middle School Expansion vote is approved by the voters of Beacon Falls again.

United Church Choir starts a singing telephone service.

Schaeffer-Fischer Post No. 25, with Oxford Post No. 174 and Seymour Post No. 10, hold an official flag service and retirement ceremony at French Memorial Field in Seymour.

April: The Beacon Falls Historical Commission presents "Beacon Falls Exposition." Twenty-three organizations and businesses participated.

June: Several hundred people turn out to welcome the Slovenian Special Olympian Delegation, whom the Town of Beacon Falls sponsored.

July: After eighteen years as First Selectman, Mr. Leonard D'Amico announces that he will not seek another term. He is the longest-sitting First Selectman in town history.

August: The Beacon Falls Girls Softball League sponsors the Third Annual Central Valley Fast Pitch League Tournament at the Pent Road Recreation Complex.

Beacon Falls officials close Matthies Park temporarily because of fire danger due to lack of rainfall.

September: Beacon Falls Historical Society presents "Ulysses S. Grant, The Man" by Mr. Al Gambone, speaker.

November: Mrs. Susan Cable becomes the first woman to be elected as First Selectman in the town of Beacon Falls.

The 125th Anniversary Committee comes out with 1996 calendars as a fundraiser. Each calendar month features an old-time photograph.

1996 April: Residents vote 23-0 to send the fifty-five-acre parcel of Matthies property to a town-wide referendum.

Spring: Laurel Ledge students gather in the school parking lot and form a large "125" in red, white and blue clothes to help the town celebrate its 125th birthday.

Mrs. Connie Christensen retires after serving thirty-nine years as librarian of the Beacon Falls Public Library—a job well done.

June 13: Beacon Falls votes on selling land to Regional School No. 16 to build a high school. Vote passes: Yes, 416, No, 330.

July: Despite rain, thousands show up to help celebrate the Quasquicentennial celebration of the town of Beacon Falls.

The United Church celebrates its 150th year in Beacon Falls (originally a Methodist congregation).

October 15: Beacon Falls and Prospect hold referendum regarding the building of a regional high school. It is rejected by more than 1,500 votes.

October 16: Beacon Falls calls for the dissolution of Regional School District No. 16 as a result of the high failed high school vote.

Fall: Masuk High School sets a two-hundred-student cap for Region No. 16. Naugatuck High agrees to enroll forty students per class. Crunch.

Representative Jack Betkoski accepts Governor Rowland's appointment to the Department of Public Utilities Control. He has chosen to give up his seat in the state legislature, one that he has held since 1986.

1997 Town of Beacon Falls files an injunction in the Milford courts against Region No. 16 to keep the school district from moving ahead with any large-scale building projects. The wording is intended to keep any high school project from being forced on Beacon Falls. This causes a big ruckus, as the wording is interpreted to mean "any building project."

November election: First Selectmen Susan Cable (D) is reelected by wide margin over Republican candidate Chris Sura.

Beacon Falls pushes for the dissolution of Regional School District No. 16. A special bill, Senate Bill #83 (SB#83), is drafted by Senator Crisco and Representative Len Greene. The legislation is worded to change the current law to allow a town within a regional school district that is without a high school to vote the school district dissolved without the other town's approval for the breakup. SB#83 passes the State Education Committee and the Senate before being defeated in the House by only twenty-one votes.

1998 New legislative session begins, with SB#83 being reintroduced to the State Education Committee. The bill emerges on March 20 as SB#205, being unanimously supported by the bipartisan Education Committee.

March 25: The Region No. 16 School Board votes to go to referendum on the Matthies site one more time. The board is split 6-2 in favor of moving to referendum. The school passes, sending the towns of Beacon Falls and Prospect into a new era.

1999 The Region No. 16 High School Building Project begins.

2001 August: Woodland Regional High School opens with its first two classes, freshman and sophomore.

BIBLIOGRAPHY

Adt, Alfred A., photographer. High Rock Grove stereograph photo. Waterbury, Connecticut.

Bailey, Paul, et al. "Tracy Lewis House 35 Wolfe Avenue Beacon Falls, Connecticut—Conditions Assessment & Reuse Study." New Haven, CT: Paul Bailey Architect, 2010.

Bonk, Mary, and Thomas Carson. *Gale Encyclopedia of U.S. Economic History*. United Kingdom: Gale Group, 1999.

The Connecticut Historical Society. *Foliage Excursion! High Rock Grove, on Saturday October 14, 1882, In Aid of the Poor Children's Fund. Grand Closing of the Season.* New Haven, CT, 1882.

DeBisschop, Dorothy. *Historical Personalities of the Lower Naugatuck Valley*. N.p., 1988.

De Forest, John W. *History of the Indians of Connecticut from the Earliest Known Period to 1850.* Hartford: Connecticut Historical Society, Wm. Jas. Hamersley, 1852.

Evening Sentinel. "Ferryboat." February 25, 1949.

FuturePast Preservation. *Industry, Eccentricity, and Engineering: A Biography of Bernard H. Matthies and a History of Matthies Park Beacon Falls, Connecticut.* Prepared for the Beacon Falls Parks and Recreation Commission. Hartford, CT, 2012.

Haas, James E. *Conrad Poppenhusen: Life of a German American Industrial Pioneer.* Baltimore, MD: Gateway Press, n.d.

Jerries, Wm. H. *Portland Transcript* 8, no. 47 (1845): 377.

Krenesky, Michael. *My Beacon Falls: A Chronological History of the Town of Beacon Falls, Connecticut.* Beacon Falls, CT: self-published, 1999.

Leuchars, Bill. "A Recreation Area—High Rock Was Once at Top of the Heap." *Waterbury Republican*, n.d.

National Society for the Preservation of Covered Bridges. "Demolition and New Construction of the Depot Street Bridge." Photograph, Michael C. Devito Collection, given by Richard Roy, former president of the NSPCB, to Michael A. Krenesky and the Beacon Falls Historical Society.

Naugatuck Daily News. "Beacon Falls Mill Sold." August 23, 1898.

———. "Fire at High Rock Grove." October 27, 1910, 1.

———. "Twenty Years Ago." July 3, 1925.

The Naugatuck Railroad Company. *High Rock Grove: A Description, Geographical, Historical Poetical, and Practical, of the Famous Picnic Ground of the Naugatuck Valley.* Boston: Franklin Press, Rand, Avery & Co., 1880.

Orcutt, Samuel. *The Indians of the Housatonic and Naugatuck Valleys.* Hartford, CT: Case, Lockwood & Brainard Company, 1882.

Ruilson, Duane. *Blue Laws of Connecticut: A Collection of the Earliest Statutes and Judicial Proceedings of That Colony Being an Exhibition of the Rigorous Morals and Legislation of the Puritains.* Philadelphia, PA: Duane Ruilson, 1861.

Steiner, Bernard C. *History of Slavery in Connecticut.* Eleventh series. Baltimore, MD: Johns Hopkins University Press, 1893.

Stephens, Joseph. *Sunday Waterbury Republican*, December 2, 1962, 6–7.

Woshner, Mike. *India-Rubber and Gutta-Percha in the Civil War Era.* Alexandria, VA: O'Donnell Publications, 1999.

About the Author

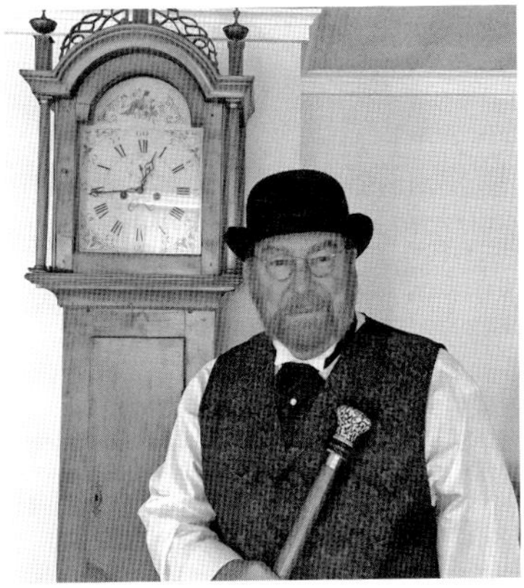

Michael Alan Krenesky is a lifelong resident of Beacon Falls, where he lives with his wife, Joyce. He is currently in his fifth term as selectman of the Town of Beacon Falls; he is also the town's municipal historian and president of the Beacon Falls Historical Society. Mike served eleven years on the Regional School District No. 16 Board of Education and two terms as the town treasurer. Mike, who spent his forty-year career working as senior project manager in the IT industry, retired in 2021. He graduated with honors from Bentley University (formerly Bentley College) in 1981. Mike has worked as a background actor in several films and had a featured background role in the CPTV series *Cobblestone Corridor* (2016). His hobbies include golf, genealogy, underwater photography and flying drones. Mike is an award-winning amateur winemaker.